PERCEPTION POWER

10 SKILLS TO GET YOUR TEAM TO BUY IN, TAKE ACTION AND GAIN MOMENTUM

Linda Shaffer-Vanaria

Disclaimer
The views expressed in Perception Power are those of the author. Although they are grounded in extensive experience, they may not be the experience of everyone that uses them. They are offered to the reader to provide an enhanced perspective on the topic of perception. The situations in this book have been generalized so they do not highlight any specific person or industry. They are provided as examples to enhance the ability to learn the concepts. Many of these examples have been witnessed similarly with many leaders and as such were chosen as they illustrate some common things that emerge in the business sector. They are illuminated as an individual to make it easy for the reader to relate to the leaders in the examples.

PERCEPTION POWER

Table of Contents

CHAPTER 2

CHAPTER 3

CHAPTER 4

CHAPTER 7

CHAPTER 8

CHAPTER 9

DEDICATION

Dedicated to leaders of global teams and organizations who want to have mastery with managing their perception in the world of 24-7

"Evolving mastery with enabling your Perception Power is essential to a reputation of peak performance with influence"

Linda Shaffer-Vanaria

PREFACE

Although I did not fully understand it at the time, the topic of *Perception Power* emerged during my days as a U.S. Navy Test Pilot. It was a world where test pilots not only flight tested various aircraft and their systems, but also one in which these same test pilots served as a team's project manager during the test's conduct. Typical flight tests would involve communicating test data to the test team for analysis; either quantitative or qualitative in nature. Accordingly, and in real-time, providing to the test team what the pilot is sensing, witnessing, and acting upon literally could mean the difference between safe execution and catastrophe. Now years later and thinking back to those days, I appreciate that the bond between test pilot and test team is one of perception management. In one instance, I recall that during a particular flight test, one of my team members detected an inflection in my voice which led to the flight's termination and for good cause; the airplane's oxygen system, unbeknownst to me, had malfunctioned and I was experiencing the onset of hypoxia. I can now appreciate that this team member's perception had been managed to the point where he knew something was afoul even before I did. Translating this story to today's workplace is why we are here. Without perception management, leaders should not expect their team, on their own, to put together all the elements in-play and predict outcomes. Rather, via *Perception Power,* actively grooming the perceptions of your team or organization, goals will be met and business disasters averted; and as was proven in my case, a safe and happy landing in the end.

Welcome to Perception Power

Welcome to PERCEPTION POWER and its invitation to spend time in evolving the perception enhancement skills critical to optimizing ongoing transition, sustainment, and transformation to your next level of achievement. PERCEPTION POWER invites you via enhancing your skills to buy-in, take action, and gain momentum to that next level.

PERCEPTION POWER BIG IDEA

PERCEPTION POWER's Big Idea is that with ongoing skill and deliberate care, perception can be honed to become a powerful agent that inspires yourself as well as others to buy in, take action, and gain momentum; leapfrogging whatever it is that you are undertaking to the next level and beyond.

Prior to embarking on my second career as an Executive Coach and Change Agent, I was a career Naval Officer and Navy Pilot. During that time while enrolled in the U.S. Naval War College, one of the things that I learned is that the results of war or aggression are never final. This thought of not being final is well applied to almost any pursuit of perishable outcomes including perception, thus, *PERCEPTION IS NEVER FINAL.* What this means is that perception is not "one and done;" rather, it is an ongoing occurrence and as such poses to each of us a requirement to be pro-active in shaping the perceptions around us to be in

1

alignment. By aligning perceptions, leaders eliminate misunderstanding and cut through the group factions and endless back-and-forth or outright stalling we have all encountered in team project management.

HOW PERCEPTION FITS INTO THE WORLD OF TODAY

We live in a world where distractions compete for our attention every eight seconds or so with those around us, and in particular, with all in the work force generally moving from moment-to-moment. As such, each previous moment becomes a blur in the process. Within this blur, leaders having the right things seen and noticed is not something we necessarily can count upon. Note that this does not mean that our people, who may or may not be noticing or capturing things observed or heard, are not competent. Rather, their competency is relative to the impacts they are focused upon creating. This is simply a statement of the state-of-the-world around us and how easy it is for things, sometimes very important things, to pass us by.

Think about what this moment-to-moment state-of-the-world means to opportunities in being in someone's thoughts; specifically, in the context that you most need and want to be in that person's thoughts? Next, think about the odds of being in that person's thoughts in a way in which he or she grasps where you fit into the strategic big picture and in the manner, you want to be seen? The message here is that by doing nothing to shape that person's perspective and perceptions, we are leaving it to chance. Leaving how people notice and absorb our message to passing chance is neither a formula for buy-in, nor enabling the taking of strategic action, nor the gaining of momentum decisively.

PERCEPTION MANAGEMENT OSMOSIS APPROACH

In coaching over a thousand leaders across a breadth of industries, roles, business environments, and levels, I have noticed a distinct pattern wherein leaders routinely communicate only in-part, falsely believing that they have actually communicated the greater picture. This I found particularly to occur when the communication is friendly and hits the mark for the conversation at-hand. When I catch leaders in this mode, which I now refer to as the *Perception Management By Osmosis Approach*, I walk them through a tour of their daily reality. I often ask them "how many emails do you have in your inbox right now?" Next, "how many emails does your boss or whatever person have in their inbox?" Then, "do you know what is in their emails and what is going on with the big picture of their communication?" And finally, "How many projects are you working on?" Does that person see the big picture of how all those projects fit together?" "How many projects are they working on? Do you have the full picture of that?" Somewhere in that daily reality tour, a light bulb goes off that good impromptu communication, although still good and still necessary, is not a sufficient perception management tool. Great briefings on technical things are still great and still necessary, but in and of themselves, do not manage perception. Rather, *if impromptu communication or prepared briefings are deliberately shaped to impart a particular message or end result take-away, they are in fact shaping the perceptions of the intended audience.* Before continuing my writing on this book early one morning and at a time when most people are on their commute to work, I stopped at a local bakery; one which off and on, I have patronized for years. Upon entering the door and rather dismayed, I noticed that there was very little remaining on the shelf. Mentioning this lack of selection to the individual behind the counter, I was told that there will only be a few more items coming out and that likely, it would be some time before they would be ready. Immediately, my perception that this bakery no longer was focused on pleasing early morning business commuters was shaped, and I considered that the bakery might have a new approach to doing business. Had the individual helping me merely stated that something popped-up for the baker that morning, my perception would have remained that they do still focus on early morning business commuters and that something emergent happened; as, at one time or another, has happened to all of us. The big picture here is that whether in basic day-to-day or circumstantial communication, we often do not understand or consider the prevailing message of perception in others that we are shaping.

Everyone knows that for plants to thrive, they must be watered. Thinking back to our high school biology classes, this process is known as osmosis, whereby water is absorbed into the plant. What would happen if we merely put the water in a cup and left it in the vicinity of the plant? We already know that answer but similarly, what if we keep our thoughts to ourselves and do not actively communicate them to those around us? The opportunity differential here is *Perception Power,* whereby deliberately, the perceptions of others can be shaped.

TAKING OWNERSHIP OF YOUR PERCEPTION CHANNEL

As a university undergraduate, I studied systems engineering and one of my labs was on signals modulation *(please don't get scared here, this won't be painful, I promise)*.

4

In signals modulation, there is a "Carrier Wave" that ensures the signal is contained like a package, while the "Modulation" within the "Carrier" provides the exact message. Respectively, the "Carrier" and "Modulation" are metaphoric to day-to-day perception management practices and the specifics of the message at hand. Think about your car's radio. First, you tune into the desired station (Carrier) which in perception management, equates to the specific person, team, or organization you intend to influence and then, listen to what that station is broadcasting (Modulation), which equates to the influencing message you are intending to communicate. Diving further into our radio station metaphor and depending upon the music being broadcast, some may focus on the music's words, its melody, or on tuning it out, completely. If a trusted friend shares that the lyrics to a particular song are moving, our perception, before even hearing the song, will align to their remarks and we will want to hear that song and share in it. Accordingly, this book is designed to help you gain structure and clarity in refining the communication of messages such that you shape others perception to be a channel of your success. This is the essence of *Perception Power*; the means by which to create buy-in and promote action-taking to achieve the desired end-result.

TOUCH POINTS ADD UP

Over the many years of coaching leaders, I have often commenced sessions where the leader shares that something seems to be working well without requiring his or her significant investment in time. Whenever I hear that, I ask "tell me about the 'Not Much' that you are doing?" One particular client comes to mind who shared that weekly, he connected with the customer and in doing so, learned the key impacts of listening to the customer and as a matter of course communicated these with his

5

team. Unknowingly, this client was shaping the perception of his entire team regarding the importance of their work. Probing further, I asked "how often do you talk to your team?" His answer, "everyday!" Next, I asked "when you talk to your team, how many are present?" "All 50," he replied. "Wow," I said, "50 people every day getting real feedback about how significant their impact is, no wonder they're excited about what they do." I then shared, that every time he talks to them, that per day, he creates 50 touchpoints in the team's understanding and appreciation of their value, 250 touchpoints per week, 1,000 touch points per month, and 12,000 touchpoints per year, not to mention the touchpoints they themselves create in influencing other teams by their energy and motivation. The significant lesson to be learned from this story is that most often, we confuse the relationship between difficulty and impact. In communication, difficulty and impact are not synonymous and in fact, it is often the most-simple forms of communication that can be the most impactful. To achieve *Perception Power*, we must be deliberate. In the above example, once I brought to the leader's attention, the impact of his communication in shaping the team's perception, he realized the power inherent in something he formerly considered trivial. The team's momentum and productivity were a direct result of their perception's shaping.

COMMITMENT TO YOUR PERCEPTION CHANNEL

To become great at most things we must evolve skills and be committed to the outcome. We have just talked about why today, perception is so important and how it often gets left to chance. To grow from this book and its learnings; lessons that bear the fruit from the experiences of over a thousand leaders before you, you must be committed. So, the question here is *Are you committed to evolving deliberately the skills and strategies necessary in managing perceptions for greater buy-in, taking action, and gaining momentum?*

There is only one answer to this question for leaders who want to be brilliant in the world of today. *That answer is Yes!*

Now that you have taken ownership of your commitment, let's walk through skills and strategies to do just that. The skills presented here are a blend of numeric, metaphoric, and structures. Evolving from my coaching practice, these skills consistently help leaders grasp what they must do in order to own perception management consistently; in bite-size, strategic, and doable ways.

CHAPTER 1

What is Perception?

"There are things known and there are things unknown,
and in between are the doors of perception."
-Aldous Huxley, "English Philosopher

RECOGNIZING DOORS OF PERCEPTION

Aldous Huxley's quote above highlights where perception is to be discovered, specifically amongst things that are known and unknown. That leaves things to interpretation. His statement alludes to the opportunity for perception to be brought into alignment or misalignment, depending upon whether or not you discover a door, choose to open, or choose to close a door. So, in building our capacity to engage with the doors of perception, we first must answer, "What exactly is a door?"

We all know that a door, physically, or in some cases symbolically, grants access. Physical doors grant access to a building, room, or closet, and they may be open, closed, or when we find ourselves in a hurry, somewhere in between. Doors may also be symbolic or metaphoric where permission must be granted for one level of understanding to be achieved, thus enabling the next level of understanding to be possible.

Regarding doors to perception, they likely are not physical doors, although a physical door may present a perception. For example, a physical door marked with warning or hazard labels presents us with the perception that what is behind it is dangerous. In fact, since it is closed, unless we ever have seen it opened, we really do not know if what is behind that door is dangerous at all, do we? Perhaps in reality, it is an empty space! Closed physical doors in the workplace may also leave us with the perception that if somebody is behind the door, they are not open to engagement at this time. Enough for now on physical doors, let's turn back to our doors of perception.

What is important with the concept of a door of perception is that we may not realize that there even is a door. In my coaching practice, I continually hear from leaders that are surprised by team members' perceptions of their leadership, as received through formal feedback. Their remarks usually go something like "how can they think _____ about me? I have an open-door policy!" Their perception of the door may be that it is truly an open door, with anyone welcome for anything, at any time, and that because their open-door policy exists, that communication will emerge a shared understanding. This view of open-door policy misses several key points that must be considered.

Point 1: In business, there is the dynamic of an ever-changing work force. Perhaps, recently there was a large personnel turnover or maybe, there are only a few new people. No matter, the question here is if everyone knows of the open door policy? Such a policy must be continuously reinforced to be effective.

Point 2: So what is this open-door policy anyway? Is it for anything, anytime? Is it only for safety related issues? Is it for everyone or only your immediate subordinates? I think you get the picture. Unless we communicate what we mean, everything, including our open-door policy, will be for naught. For example, imagine someone in your division with something they want to share. They even know that there is an open-door policy but they still are a bit unsure. "Will I be a bother? What type of reaction will I get? I'm only the messenger, but will I be the one to get shot?" Realize it or not, these types of concerns exist in every organization, and can only be addressed via perception management.

There is an even greater challenge with open-door policies. When someone comes to the door that is open, they are coming typically to ask something, or seek information or opinions about which they are unsure. As such, the open door is indeed open, but the content flowing through the door is reactive, meaning that in order to know it or share it, they had to come to the door.

So let's now consider the whole open-door policy thing to begin with. Again, what was the intent? Rather than via an open-door policy, could we not create greater trust and understanding amongst our team by being proactive in our communication, such that routinely, there is no need to seek out an open door? We could then maintain a certain amount of trust and shared vision and the open-door policy could become one of spontaneous need.

Regarding doors to perception, these must occur in such a way that people know they are there, want to use them, are willing to use them, and artfully and wisely, are able to use them. As children, we learn to open physical doors. As adults, we learn to open the *Gateway Doors of Perception* in our professional work, where the door entered becomes a gateway to clarity, mutual understanding, and evolving perceptions, to those that enhance relationships and outcomes. As with anything, the better our awareness, skills, and strategies are honed, the more effective we will be.

Facilitating leaders in *Recognizing Doors of Perception* that are in their midst is the intent of the skills to be presented in this book. Specifically, insights into the possibilities to promote buy in, taking action, and gaining momentum with your teams, organizations, and within the context of your life, will be discussed. The primary audience here are leaders, whether team, small business, or large corporation, but such skills readily can spill over to commanding results in all arenas of our lives.

TAKING CHARGE OF YOUR VIRTUAL DOOR

When we think of a door, typically, we think of a door that we are engaging physically, perhaps at home or in a real office setting. What is critical to realize in the world today, specifically the global world of 24/7, is that so much of our communication is accomplished through virtual doors via one or multiple forms of electronic media. Today, we may even be communicating with robots (or, if you're in-the-know, with a "bot").

One area I learned about, during my first career as a Navy Pilot, is that of composites. Composite materials are compositions of mixed substances, which bring both strength and flexibility to aircraft design. Similarly, our doors of perception today must be composites of face-to-face, virtual engagement, and virtual reality. If we fail to think of these doors of perception as the doors that they are, we will fail to notice and act upon opportunities and quite rather, we will live in a reactionary world. The questions here, then are "What doors do I have that are already open?" and "What doors do I need to open (or perhaps close)?" Also, it will be important to consider what may or may not be included in these doors? Our tone, style, willingness to engage, and approach will all be part of what shapes our doors of perception.

RECOGNIZING THE MANY INTERFACES OF PERCEPTION

Once we find the doors to perception, it then is important to know perception when we see, experience, or witness it. Here, a basic definition of perception will be required before getting started. *Perception is often defined as a mental impression or way of regarding something. Perception is often described in terms of our five senses; how we see, smell, taste, hear, or feel something* (or, if you're into the leadership or psychology realm, it includes our sixth sense, *intuition*). Perception is both an element, all its own, as well as something intertwined with mindset, feedback, and perspective. My intent is not to present these things as academic concepts, where you will get tested on how they interface. Rather, the intent here is to provide leaders with a basic awareness of these interfaces to such a degree that they may be leveraged in managing your own perception as well as those of your team. To do this well requires thought and proactivity.

Next we are presenting a model that shows the key perception interfaces. The intention of the model is to help you to visualize the perception interfaces with how the interfaces relate to the perceptions you are managing, and also to each of the other interfaces. We will now walk through these interfaces one-by-one to enhance your clarity on how they relate to managing perception. The intention is for you be mindful of these interfaces before we begin talking about the 10 skills for PERCEPTION POWER.

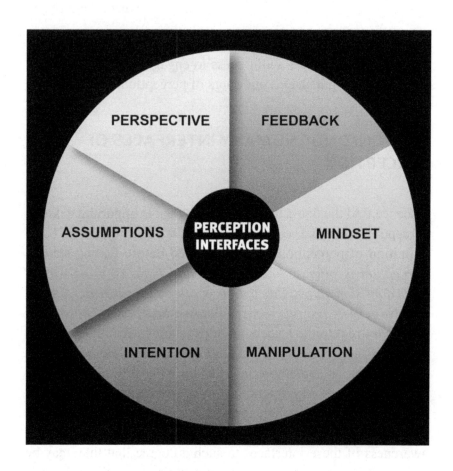

WHERE PERCEPTION MEETS FEEDBACK

Feedback is one of those things that we often do not spend much time considering, beyond it being essential and needing to ask for some. Feedback is essential as a leader, person, parent, and in every role of our lives. It is essential not only to embrace giving and receiving feedback, but also to understand how we invite feedback.

In engendering feedback, it must be understood that people expect that what they share will be met with respect, consideration, and appreciation. They do not necessarily expect you to embrace what it is that they are saying, although likely, they truly hope for that. Why, as leaders this is important to internalize, is that we often do not ask for others' feedback or perspectives, because we fear being expected to do exactly what others think we should do. Also, in receiving feedback, we know that we may not be able or want to do what was asked, nor feel what was asked is wise.

As such, in leveraging feedback as an alignment tool, where people will want, but may not expect you to do certain things, a door to perception will actually be opened. Here, a need for dialogue between the leader (feedback recipient) and his or her team (feedback givers) exists and therefore, an opportunity to manage perspectives, for both leader and team, also exists. That said, I cannot overemphasize that providers of feedback do hope that their feedback recipients will act upon the feedback as well as loop-back to them with what was done.

Feedback givers may want a key action or transformation in your viewpoint or perspective. If you are not ready to act now, they may hope that you keep their feedback in your queue for consideration later. The perception you create by listening and closing the loop with the feedback provider is that their perspective is important to you. When someone feels important, they feel empowered and are more likely to keep the feedback loop flowing. This ensures that a leader becomes aware of risks, and opportunities, and even blind spots.

In short, they learn why they should care and what needs to be done. You are in essence, with the vehicle of feedback, enabling others to understand and embrace how you need and want them to think, feel, and act in such a way that the feedback loop can continue to connect the dots and refine perceptions. Where perception fits in with feedback is in enabling others to consider and embrace your focus: specifically, the "who, what, where, why and how" of its fit in the big picture.

WHERE PERCEPTION MEETS MINDSET

Perception is part of a mindset and it is also an element unto itself. Mindset includes the composite of assumptions, perspectives, focal elements, and prevailing attitudes. Individuals can have a business mindset, get it done mindset, or some combination of mindsets, and flow back and forth amongst them. Perception can trigger someone into or out of a mindset, so it is a very powerful instrument in shaping how others engage and work with us. Note that we are not here to debate whether something is a perception or a mindset; rather the intent is to recognize that perception and mindset are in the blend of what is being thought about and acted upon. When setting out to manage perceptions, a leader may share their perspectives on mindset and how they hope them to be perceived. When a leader speaks to a certain mindset and invites his team to think from that mindset, a common perception aligned to the desired outcomes will be shaped.

WHERE PERCEPTION MEETS PERSPECTIVE

Perspective in art is about giving something depth and making it feel real. In writing and conversation, perspectives are often described as points-of-view; bringing a deeper sense of understanding to what is being discussed or debated. We can look at an object or a situation from several perspectives or points-of-view, thereby emerging our own informed perspective, now drawing upon a deeper awareness of several perspectives. Our perception may or may not be logically informed. It may be informed emotionally or in reaction to our senses.

The opportunity with *Perception Power* is to develop skills that enlighten how we leverage perspectives to engender perceptions that create enhanced buy-in, taking-of-action, and gaining-of-momentum. As with perspective in fine art, taking perception management to an art form requires refined skills. Over the course of this book, we will focus on developing those skills and moving your perception management to a refined art form, thus building your *Perception Power.*

WHERE PERCEPTION MEETS MANIPULATION

Through client engagement, I have learned that when leaders begin work on new behaviors; particularly those behaviors surrounding perception management, they often raise concerns of becoming phony or manipulative. As such, it is critical to pause and touch base with this concern. Being manipulative means trying to force people into something that is not truthful or beneficial to themselves, their team, or organization. What is essential to internalize here is that when living to our highest values, we may be called to perform outside of our individual comfort zones. In some cases, this may trigger a feeling of phoniness, until such time that you check-in with your discomfort and what it means to the bigger picture. This check-in requires consciousness and deliberateness or we likely may bypass the surrounding opportunity. Realize here that the reason you might feel odd, phony, or unnatural is that you embarking upon a new area or one in which you have yet to form natural habits. As a rule of thumb, it takes doing things several times before becoming comfortable; let-alone the consistency required for it to become habitual!

Think of things we do to make ourselves comfortable that are not good for us or in our best interest, and how they relate to perception. We may feel comfortable eating a bag of chocolate. This does not mean that our perception is that eating a bag of chocolate is in our best interest. So, as you are working through the skills presented in the following chapters that might feel new or odd, pause to reorient yourself and be open to the fact that new habits, approaches, and consciousness to move yourself forward may be required. Once you get the hang of these skills and how to employ them, you naturally will move from the skills being counter-intuitive to becoming intuitive and as such, an inherent part of your natural repertoire.

WHERE PERCEPTION MEETS INTENTION

An intention prescribes a goal, aim, or end-game. It does so from a place of emotional conviction to achieve its fulfillment. When I first set out to join the Navy, my intention was to find a pathway to become a pilot. My perception was that it might not be possible because U.S. Code Title 10 restrictions at the time did not allow women in combat. Because of the depth of my intention and conviction, I kept searching for perspectives and answers on how to manifest my intention into reality. During the unfolding journey, my perceptions and perspectives emerged and evolved. I invited the shaping of my perception and perspectives from others and also shaped the perception of myself to others in the process. Over the ensuing years, I came to realize increasingly why perception management skills would be crucial in bringing intent to reality. This realization led to my manifesting mentors, finding influencers, and creating belief in my capability to take on roles that could position myself for aspirational opportunities, all to champion my career pathway.

WHERE PERCEPTION MEETS ASSUMPTIONS

Assumptions are things that are taken to be true without any specific proof. They are things which we believe to be grounded, with no requirement for a time-out to look at the specific data. We might assume that someone knows what they are doing with a specific task. We may further assume this to be the case because we have not heard anything to the contrary. Assumptions may also be founded based upon cultural norms or things we have learned. We usually make assumptions with little or no information from any of our senses. In contrast, typically, perceptions are extensions of information from our senses, while assumptions are not.

The above is not about debating whether something is a perception or an assumption, because both are important influencers. Rather, it is about realizing that to inform our perceptions, first, it is good to check in on our own and others assumptions and then second, to evaluate which doors we must open or close in evolving our perceptions to the point that can enable strategic gain via buy in, taking action, and gaining momentum.

A STORY OF MANAGING MY DOOR AS A SQUADRON COMMANDING OFFICER

One of the things that I became very aware of, when I assumed responsibility as a Squadron Commanding Officer (CO), was a perception that the CO's door was selectively open, unless by the CO, positioned otherwise. My squadron's perception was that as their new CO, I could hold them accountable, therefore creating a natural reluctance to come and share things with me. I wanted the people that worked for me to believe that the door to conversations critical to our squadron would always be open. In particular, anything related to squadron safety and mission accomplishment needed to be discussed openly and without fear of reprisal. Additionally, I also would welcome any conversations in leading my people effectively as well as helping them in some way. One "ice-breaker" I implemented right away was to stock a candy dish with the favorite candy of each of my department heads, placing it at my office entry door. I wanted my department heads to have a reason in dropping by to talk as well as for them to perceive that they were invited. I also realized that I could not assume that people were asking me the questions that they wanted to ask. So I would casually ask varied questions and keep a curious face to listen to their answers. In retrospect, all of these things paid dividends. In reflecting about this story of my past and the skills here, I realize that with some of additional skills I have since learned, and which I now detail in this book, I could have opened doors of perception even further.

INTRODUCING THE PERCEPTION POWER MODEL

Now that we have discussed "What is Perception?" including the doors to perception and Perception Interfaces model, you are ready to be introduced to the PERCEPTION POWER Skills Model presented next. This model shows you each of the skills that you will learn. We will go through each skill one by one clockwise starting with STORY. Think of the model like an orange where each slice is great in and of itself but in order for it to be an orange you must have all the slices. The goal is to become masterful at each skill so you can experience benefits of PERCEPTION POWER in enhancing buy in, taking action and gaining momentum.

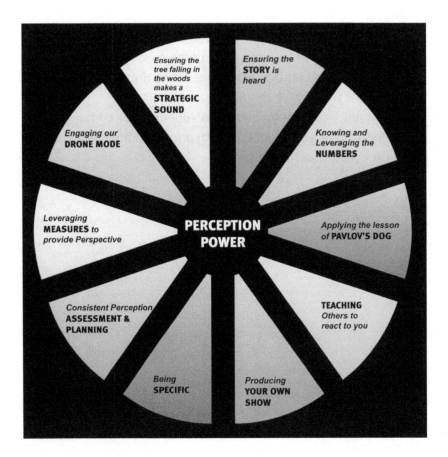

CALL TO ACTION

It is important as you step through the concepts and skills of PERCEPTION POWER to pause to absorb them so you can use them immediately. The pause to absorb the concepts will also enable you to readily add what you are learning with new skills onto what you have learned previously. So the end of each chapter will have a CALL TO ACTION. Your CALL TO ACTION with "What is Perception?" is to explore/do the following:

1. Reflect upon, "What are your doors of perception?"
2. Reflect upon, "How can you become more deliberate in identifying and taking ownership of the doors of perception available to you?"
3. What practices can you begin to support your taking ownership of your doors of perception and how you work with Perception Interfaces?

CHAPTER 2

SKILL ONE: Ensuring the Story is Heard

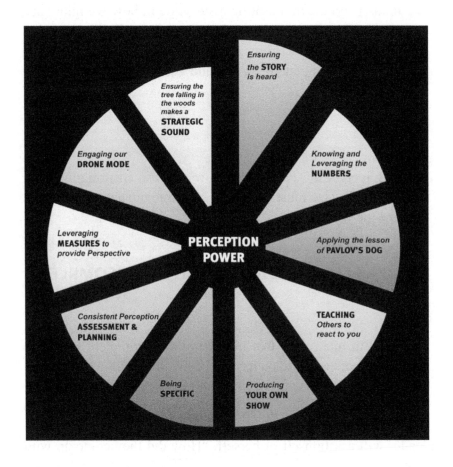

The concept of communicating through stories is as old as culture itself. You would think that by today, mastery in the art of communicating stories would be inherent in one's DNA. Sadly, this is not the case. We all have heard, appreciated, and told stories, but what must be introduced here is a key skill in managing perception via the art of storytelling, such that the story's elements are communicated and heard in the manner in which intended. This is not about the kind of stories that mesmerize and entertain, although, these may be a subset. Rather, the focus is on communicating a storyline in how we think, act, react, intend, and feel, and how the dots connect from end-to-end. These stories acknowledge and transform perception, creating capacity for buy in, taking action, and gaining momentum.

BIG IDEA

The Big Idea of the *Perception Power* skill in ensuring the story is heard is that we must create the storyline to shape how others witness the world with us.

UNDERSTAND THE IMPACT OF THE INCOMPLETE STORY

We need to internalize that in sharing an incomplete story, we cannot expect the world on its own magically to fill in the rest and reach the conclusion that we want to impart. That simply will not happen. People simply may form an impression or attempt to complete the story based on what was shared, where upon the leader will ask himself or herself, "How did they come up with that?"

EXAMPLE OF THE IMPACT OF AN INCOMPLETE STORY

Several years ago, I coached a client just after she had received her 360-degree feedback. She was very irate about what her boss had shared about her with regard to her having a limited strategic understanding. During our session and with all the emotions of upset, anger, and sheer frustration, she enumerated to me a litany of all she had accomplished and why, along with the positive impact each item had made. I remarked to her that "These are some pretty impressive things that you are telling me, have you shared these with your boss?" She proceeded to explain to me that her organization's approach to meetings did not allow for her to communicate her accomplishments. So after listening to her frustration and upset for having done all these remarkable things that she was sharing with me and not being appreciated for, I remarked "I think I'm starting to understand what's going on, you're mad at your boss for not knowing what you never told him." Her reaction was amazing. She went from being upset to laughing at the pie in her face from our reality check.

Continuing with the session, I pointed out that "I get that the meetings that you go to do not allow for sharing all these things you shared with me, but for instance does he read email when it is sent to him? Are there other ways of sharing these types of things for the message to be transmitted? Is there a way of getting your own unique meeting with him once in a while where you could set a tone via sharing different content? Is there a way of sharing some strategic works once in a while that could showcase your strategic philosophy, engagement, and follow through? Perhaps, when you get an email on some topic, you could add some additional content to keep the storyline flowing, as for example "Oh, by the way, on this, just want you to know that dah-dah-dah is going on and we are really excited about how it is hitting the mark on this strategic initiative."

Now, she realized that there could be a whole series of ways of actually managing the different perception elements of her unfolding strategic engagement. No surprise, when she took this to heart and worked on ensuring she shared the full story of her strategic engagement, her boss and everyone else noted her storyline as operationally strategic and recognized her as a key player.

ENSURING YOUR CHAPTERS ARE IN YOUR STORY

I have noticed a theme of leaders not taking time to think about the contexts that are expressed in their communication. *By context, I mean anything that helps a story to be understood in the manner in which its originator intends it to be understood.* Typically, leaders, in a reactionary way, respond to most communications as "answering the mail." As such, leaders are not taking time to ensure that their communication is proactively shaped and producing a full picture of any given situation. Think how often we receive a short email or text that speaks to us in chat form; something similar to "Joe, what's up with _____ (whatever the topic)?" Joe then responds back, "It's going fine." Typically, in answering the mail, we do not pause and reflect upon, "what do I need to add here to make sure he or she sees the 'whatever' in the way in which I want it to be seen and understood? There is a prevailing tendency to leave out the contexts which help shape that shared interpretation. When this happens, we find ourselves mad or irritated with the person to whom we communicated in not fully appreciating our efforts and the outcomes.

To ensure your story is fully communicated in a way that it is understood, specifically the way it needs to and must be understood, mandates that we must be willing to ensure the storyline is complete. We must ensure that all the chapters are in the story.

The majority of leaders do not fully communicate their story. In working with these leaders, I ask them to imagine being given a book that has 30 chapters, but for the sake of expediency, I ripped out chapters 3, 11, and 16. They could still generally follow the plot of the book to its end and with a solid understanding of most characters in the story. What would be missed though are the nuances of a particular character which only are described in chapter three. Perhaps this character, earlier identified as gruff and looking like a villain was really an ally, learned only in one of the torn-out chapters. The question here, is *"What is your approach to ensure you keep all the chapters in your story?"*

IMPACT OF YOUR NOT WANTING TO BE IN THE WEEDS

One of the reasons I have observed that leaders feel compelled to leave out content is that they want to provide crisp communication. They miss the point and opportunity that a story with the right contexts need not be long. It does however need to possess the key contexts necessary in providing that a particular message be understood. Often, leaders share with me that they "do not want to get into the weeds" and as such, they avoid providing detail. To a degree, that is wise, but to the degree where key elements in the storyline are lost is foolishness.

By all means, leaders should not lose themselves in the weeds, but also, they should not attempt to communicate a picture at street level from 30,000 feet! In working with clients concerned about being down, in the weeds, I ask them to reflect upon the differences between weeds, plants, flowers, and herbs in ancient times, considering "what ultimately determines whether something got called a weed or not?" Think about it; if it was pretty, it might have been referred to as a flower. If it was useful in cooking or medicine, it may have been called an herb. If the individual or group did not like the way it looked or did not know what to do with it, it became a weed. Over the course of thousands of years, some weeds became flowers, some flowers became weeds, and some weeds became herbs. The point here is that it is all within the lens of the beholder and the context. The word that this points to is "relevance." What helps get us down to the granularity of the right details is the realization that we are not in search of details; rather we are in search of "key specifics." Key specifics are those elements key to the storyline. Sometimes there may be quite a few "key specifics." In the end, we need as many as we need, no more and no less.

A COUPLE OF KEY SPECIFICS CAN CHANGE YOUR PERCEIVED STORY

Years back, I coached a leader who was an experienced strategic expert. When he received his 360-degree feedback for leadership development, the feedback reflected that he was weak in strategy. Obviously, he was very upset about it. At the time, this leader was in a very operational role, and when asked how he ran his meetings, he stated "Bottom line, up-front." Accordingly, the challenge I gave him was to "Put some top line up-front in there too, so that the strategic elements get linked in." It was simple for him to do so and include strategic connection to the storyline in his other communications. To him, the distinction between doing strategic planning as an event and threading strategic context in day-to-day communications was transformational.

YOUR STORY MUST BE A PRIORITY AND NOT DESIGNATED AS SOMETHING EXTRA TO DO

You likely are juggling many balls at any given time, so likely, doing something extra is not your goal. What is important to realize is that often, things that are important to our communication and roles as leaders and team members can feel as extra load, because we have not done them regularly. Taking ownership of ensuring your story gets heard as you need it and most want it to be must become a priority so as not to leave it to chance. The transition we are talking about here is one of moving from simply answering the mail to communicating your storyline each and every time. Mastery here will require a small time investment but trust me, it will be worth it!

TAKE THE 5 MINUTE CHALLENGE

In my coaching practice, I continuously encounter leaders who routinely share that they do not have time to think about anything because they are too busy. Most even think that they need some form of a multi-day retreat to facilitate meaningful thought. Often, I will probe them with "We have a little time here; what do you need to think about?" I will then give them a free two minutes to think out loud with the offer that I will add an idea or two into the mix. Interestingly, I have discovered a phenomenon where leaders become uncomfortable after 20 to 25 seconds and stop thinking. With the many leaders I have given this opportunity, I have not had one use the full two minutes on their first attempt. When leaders become aware of this and give themselves permission every day to take what I now call the 5-minute challenge; investing in thinking about themselves and their communication, I have over and again witnessed profound transformational change in their sense and satisfaction of pro-active accomplishment.

A topic I invite leaders to consider during one of their 5-minute challenges is what he or she needs to communicate in promoting enhanced awareness of their storyline. Here, they learn that there is no substitute for communicating clarity on what they are accomplishing. Their storyline contexts can be wide-ranging including emotional context, historical context, process context, what happened yesterday context, and successes context, to name a few. These contexts, when clearly communicated, are the chapters comprising the story to be heard and understood in the manner desired.

The impact of this investment is the capacity to share your story under virtually any circumstance, perhaps impromptu in a hallway, when running to a meeting or while in line for a second cup of morning coffee. In each case, it is the enhancement of your capacity to manage perception and engender buy-in, the taking of action, and the gaining of momentum.

BUILD SUPPORTING STRUCTURES TO CAPTURING YOUR STORY

Supporting yourself in building mastery to ensure your story is heard in the manner in which you desire people to understand it needs be deliberate and can be simple. You might create a list of questions to organize yourself rapidly, regarding how to capture key specifics as well as thoughts on how to share them succinctly. Key questions might include: "How do I need people to understand this? What must they understand to enable ____? What do I need to include to enable them to understand the story that way?" The thoughts produced can be just a few sentences that connect the dots of key specifics.

Another example of a simple supporting structure is to have a list of contexts that you need to include in response to communications. For example, such context may include describing the team's emotional frame with "all here are overwhelmed due to ____" or "all here are excited about how we are collaborating on evolving ____." There could be a context centered on location which describes how and why things are coming together in the particular location and the approach used in that area to bring about the results witnessed. This type of context is particularly useful in influencing leadership with a sense of comfort and belief that projects in remote locations are proceeding smoothly. What is important here is that although it seems obvious to take charge of your storyline, when you are busy and doing your business as usual, it may go unnoticed until you sit down and think about it or strategically garner feedback.

How will you take ownership in ensuring your story is heard the way you most need it and want it to be understood? How will you champion your storyline to be engender perception?

CALL TO ACTION

Your CALL TO ACTION with **SKILL ONE: Ensuring the Story is Heard** is to explore/do the following:

1. Reflect upon, "How do you ensure all the chapters are in your story?"
2. Take Action on the 5 Minute Challenge.
3. Reflect upon, "What supporting structures can you build to capture your story to enable you to build your PERCEPTION POWER?"

CHAPTER 3

SKILL TWO: Knowing and Leveraging the Numbers

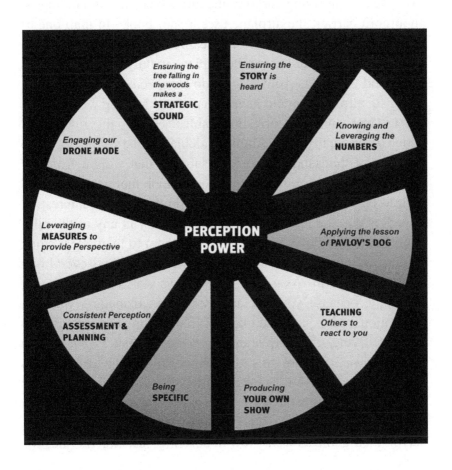

Many sports and businesses alike employ benchmarks; numbers that must be learned or even lived by in gauging success. Back in my flying days, knowing the numbers was an essential part of being a professional pilot. Several numbers simply had to be memorized to the point of immediate recall in monitoring the airplane's safety such as the engine's maximum temperature, minimum oil pressure, and fuel-burn rate. Other numbers emerged as "rules-of-thumb" to make flying a mission easier. One rule-of-thumb that I particularly remember was the "rule-of-11," used when flying cargo to the aircraft carrier. In landing on an aircraft carrier, the airplane uses a "tail hook" to grab one of the ship's three or four "arresting cables," taking the place of a long runway in order to stop the airplane in only two seconds and using and 344 feet, from a touchdown speed of 130 knots. In doing so, airplanes would have a maximum landing weight so as not to over-stress the arresting cables. Hence, the rule-of-11, which was actually quite simple. Calculating the weight of cargo in terms of thousands of pounds, subtract that weight from the number 11, and the remainder was how much fuel you could land with to be within safe weight landing limits. What is interesting though is that the rule-of-11 was not formally in any of the pilot manuals. It was cleverly devised by one pilot to facilitate a quick landing weight calculation. Soon, it was shared and everybody used it henceforth! As a pilot, you always welcomed something so simple because you are already busy in managing weather, navigation, radios, and the like, not to mention your primary job of just flying the airplane; *trust me, "busy" can be an understatement!* From this experience, the value of rules-of-thumb really stand out to me and I have searched for them ever since. Such numbers have served in keeping me in the game with whatever I am engaged in and have also served me to help others stay in their game as well. Now in coaching leaders, via rules-of-thumb, I have emerged ways of championing them to understand *Perception Power*. Similar to how the rule-of-11 was shared, the *Perception Power* numbers presented here serve as guidelines to keep you on the playing field in managing perceptions and can leapfrog you, with momentum and results, to the next level.

BIG IDEA

The Big Idea with *Knowing and Leveraging the Numbers* is that rule-of thumb numbers can, in real-time, create wins for you in the world of perception. The rule-of-thumb numbers here should be used with frequency to focus perception and enhance impact, engendering buy-in, taking of action, and gaining of momentum. Below is a model which highlights the five rules of thumb for enhancing your PERCEPTION POWER.

FIVE RULES OF THUMB	
#1 RULE	4 - 6 Rule (Communicate Perception Management Messages At Least Every 4 to 6 Weeks)
#2 RULE	The Meter Maid Rule (Become Your Own Perception Management Meter Maid)
#3 RULE	The 7 - 12 Rule (Monitor Your Communicating Key Messages At Least 7 to 12 Times)
#4 RULE	The Rule of 50 (50 Touchpoints to get to Long Term Memory)
#5 RULE	The 4 - 8 Rule (Create the capacity to manage perception via providing At least 4 to 8 perspectives)

Rule-of-Thumb #1: *The 4 – 6 Rule*

Communicate Perception Management Messages At Least Every 4 to 6 Weeks

Over the years, I have read hundreds of articles and papers on communicating across every walk of business and life. In doing so, I noticed a common thread of suggesting communication monthly, a theme that came from experience but without explanation. In today's global world of email, instant messaging, and social media, there are so many things competing for your attention that constant disruption has become the new norm. Our brains are put to the test in absorbing information. After about 4 - 6 weeks of absorbing what some studies report as 160,000 different pieces of information on a nominal day, it is not hard to imagine that the brain's hard drive is full. Thus, at the 4 – 6 week point, our brains will categorize as unimportant and naturally press "Delete" on any information that has not been heard in a while. Yes, this may be overly simplistic, yet if we think about our own capacity to retain information, it serves as a reminder to realign our own perceptions and think about what we want to share with others. We will cover more about how to leverage this opportunity when we discuss the skill of taking ownership for influencing what people think, feel, and act. For now though, employ *The 4 – 6 Rule* to ensure that others do not hit "Delete" on information you consider important in shaping their perceptions.

A REALIZATION ABOUT OUR BRAIN'S RECYCLE BIN

Many realizations come to us because of our experience and situation. One day, I was sitting back in my seat in coaching a client on the telephone. My computer was open with some documents on screen pertinent to the leader I was coaching. The documents did not fill up the whole screen, so many of the desktop icons were still visible. The sun came through the window and was beaming on the Recycle Bin icon and as such, caught my attention. What I realized in that moment while coaching a leader to manage their perception, was that our brains were more amazing than our computers in every way but one. With our computer, we can go through the Recycle Bin and verify that in fact, we want to delete an item before its actual deletion. Conversely, with our brain, once we hit delete, we do not get a second chance with a recycle bin. Rather, once deleted, something consciously has to trigger our brains to recover the item. With that thought in mind, when we are perception managing we are bringing meaning to the information that people may have observed or heard. We must actively manage perception and connect the dots, in putting meaning into the context where the proverbial lightbulbs in others can illuminate.

Rule-of-Thumb #2: The Meter Maid Rule

Become Your Own Perception Management Meter Maid

Several years ago, I took my daughter to a late afternoon doctor's appointment. The doctor's office was located on a street with parking meters. We emerged from her appointment at about 5:55 PM; five minutes before parking became free for the evening until the next morning. Right there was a meter maid, slapping tickets on all the cars that had either allowed their meters to expire a few minutes too soon, or parked their cars a few minutes too early for the free period until the next morning. This really left an impression on me regarding paying attention to the meters and erring just-in-case, to pay for a little extra time. As with so many of the events we experience, we ponder them in how they fit with other events in our lives. For me, that pondering linked to helping leaders understand the significance of feeding the perception management meter at least every 4 - 6 weeks so that their meter would not expire. By this, we mean that the perceptions in others that leaders have worked deliberately to shape will expire, unless at least at the 4 – 6 week point, they are re-fed.

I have heard leaders talk about their great quarterly meetings on occasion when amidst coaching, I probed them on how they got their information and communicated their messages. When asked about how his team communicated outside the quarterly meetings, one of my clients remarked, "Nothing, our quarterly meetings are so good that we do not need any additional communication." Interestingly, right after that remark, he stated that "what is odd though, is that all of our quarterly meetings really cover the same or similar content." We then talked about building a consistent communications flow such that there would be a perception created regarding how results of the quarterly meeting were being applied and then how to target its action items and deliverables to a next level of success, rather than rehash the same things as a matter of routine.

I also remember a client who shared that he had worked on something very diligently and it worked for a while and then stopped working. I told him that I was curious about whether he shared what he was working on a few months ago, achieved results, but then got busy and had not shared much since. He replied, "Yes, that about summarizes what happened." When I told him that "your perception management meter expired," he started laughing.

We have all attended meetings where something important, perhaps with a deadline was promulgated, only to be followed by a period of high intensity, where we lost track of time. Weeks or even months later, someone might bring up that approaching deadline, recounting that this information was distributed at such and such a meeting, whereupon, you realize that it slipped your mind until you heard mention of it again. We all do not intentionally forget these things, rather and quite simply, we need connectivity to maintain awareness.

Rule-of-Thumb #3: *The 7 - 12 Rule*

Monitor Your Communicating Key Messages at Least 7 to 12 Times

I was standing in the convention hall of a hotel amidst many colleagues while at a large conference. I happened to be stretching with a few dance exercises as I was stiff from long periods of sitting. This spawned a conversation with a colleague who also was a fan of doing such exercises repetitively. The conversation then branched into discussing the repetitions required for people to acknowledge and remember something that we share with them as coaches and leaders. Seven to 12 times was the number we were discussing that came from things we read and had learned from marketing. I now use this range as a rule-of-thumb. The point here is that it is not once, twice or even three times that we must reinforce messages; typically, the point where we think we are becoming a broken record. Quite the opposite in fact; 7 – 12 touch points are normally what it takes, adequately to communicate our messages.

I have seen with some frequency, leaders who are frustrated by the feedback they are receiving. When inquiring into how many times they have shared their message, they will often in an intense, irritated, and raised voice say "Two or Three!!!" I will then share "that is a good start but you have a long way to go." In today's environment, thousands of messages compete for our attention. Therefore, does it not make sense that messages not repeatedly reinforced will become lost? Here, knowing that repetitive communication is necessary to having our communication remembered and acted upon demonstrates that as leaders, we are not being ignored, rather, we simply are in a communications competition with everyone else and via the *7 – 12 Rule,* our communications will win!

One final point to be made regarding the *7 – 12 Rule* is that each time, our points of communication do not have to be exactly the same. For example, you have one touch point in a 3-hour meeting where you remark about _____. Then walking back to your office and conversing with others on your team, you add "I hear what you are saying. That goes with _____ that we were just discussing during the meeting." This is about bringing a sense of importance to the topic through threaded conversations. A next touch point may be in response to an email on another topic where you add in a thought related to your message. These differing touch points can happen very rapidly and in short communications which are added into the mix of other naturally occurring conversations, emails, texts, or even social media. When clear on what we need people to be thinking about and what perceptions we want and need them to have or reinforce, we can then leverage the *7 - 12 Rule* to influence their thoughts, processes, and actions.

Rule-of-Thumb #4: *The Rule of 50*

50 Touchpoints to get to Long Term Memory

The Rule of 50 emerged in conversation with the colleague mentioned above on discussing the repetitions needed for someone to acknowledge and remember something that we share with them. What emerged in that conversation was something she learned from an associate who performed research on how many touches it takes to achieve someone's long-term memory. Her research revealed the number to be 47 hits. So, for ease of our own memory, let's round that number up to 50 and hence, *The*

Rule of 50. Such a large number to be retained in long-term memory? This message, regarding the effort we must invest to ensure our message stays viable, truly is profound.

In considering *The Rule of 50*, the truth is that the impact all depends on the circumstances of who you are talking with, what the situation is, what is at stake, the cultural considerations, and a number of other variables. Also, can *The Rule of 50* vary? Absolutely! With a willing partner or audience, you may be successful with a smaller number of touches yet with the curmudgeon, it may take 100 touches! Having a rule of thumb keeps us moving toward the target of ensuring that we achieve *Perception Power*. I have ever since used *The Rule of 50* as a target and shared this with those I coach, who ask, "Well, how many times do I have to communicate it?" I now see clients leverage this number to keep them on their journey.

Rule-of-Thumb #5: *The 4-8 Rule*

Create the capacity to manage perception via providing at least 4 to 8 perspectives

In the intense world of business, leaders are trying to get things done quickly and tend for fast communication; tactically and in short blurts. When having a varying viewpoint with a concept or approach, I see a tendency for clients simply to respond back with the contrary viewpoint and what they believe is more in alignment. Immediately, this creates that very difficult environment to transcend, commonly referred to as "us versus them," or perhaps "this versus that." "Us versus them" is an environment where people, almost innately, dig their heels in to defend their point of view. Coming to mind here is my first pet dog, a rather cute but quite stubborn miniature wire-haired dachshund. In taking him to the veterinarian for boarding, although a little dog, he considered himself to be quite the big boy. He did not enjoy being boarded and at the door to the veterinarian's office, he would protest. He would sit, dig in his paws, and not budge one inch! To my dog, this was not "us versus them," it was singularly "me versus them!" "Okay," the assistants would say, "we'll carry you." If my dog realized that by being boarded, he could eat while I was gone, perhaps he would have entered the office under his own power with an "OK, I know you'll come get me. It's not my favorite place, but I'll manage while you're gone." Of course, he did not know those kinds of things (he was a dog). We however are humans with the capacity for a fuller perspective and quite frankly, with well-crafted communication, we have the power to prevent or at the very least to defuse "us" or "me versus them."

Leaders get frustrated with the fighting in "us" or "me versus them" and most often, upon perceiving that their points are not being heard or acknowledged, quit fighting, challenging others, or in the extreme give-up, feeling disempowered and unappreciated. The cost could be enormous and will extinguish innovative thinking and ultimately, the long-term success and resiliency of an organization. The points here are twofold: (1) The outlier who cries that "the emperor has no clothes" may in fact be the right voice in the room and (2) Even if not correct, the outlier, to continue functioning as a vital member of any team or organization, must perceive that he or she is being heard and upon analysis, although a different decision or outcome was reached, contrary to that which he or she expressed, their input was and will continue to be considered as of value.

In studying models of coaching and communication, there were often exercises inviting looking at things from many viewpoints.

What I realized in conducting these exercises is that if we have two views on the table, we have created "us versus them." If we put a third perspective in the mix, we create the view that there is a compromise perspective. If we put four or more views on the table, we create a landscape of perspectives where the listener is driven to consider that "Wow, there is more to this than I thought, so let's get a time on the calendar to discuss this in more detail." Knowing this offers a huge opportunity in managing perception and engendering buy-in, taking action, and gaining momentum. It makes it possible strategically to bypass the "us versus them" conversation and be perceived as a big picture thinker who looks at everything without taking sides.

Back to our outlier. . . As discussed above, pivotal to someone with a perspective is to know they are heard and that their viewpoint is acknowledged. If we acknowledge their viewpoint amongst a sharing of 4 - 8 key perspectives; *The 4 – 8 Rule,* they see the value of their perspective being heard, where it sits with others, and that there was an inclusive decision-making process. Very frequently, the perspective landed upon will be some blend of the perspectives offered.

As a leader, via *The 4 – 8 Rule,* you have the opportunity to share multiple perspectives in championing listeners to understand alternative pathways and their potential importance. This takes a little practice and some initial patience but once you get the hang of it, it becomes very doable in real-time. When you can readily engage in this manner, whether in conversation or electronic media, it becomes a reliable vehicle for managing perception. The tendency I find in clients is to believe that such an approach need take a lot of time. In truth, it is about adding a sentence or two to each viewing point. The question then becomes if you are willing to invest an extra few minutes in conversation or written form to achieve building *Perception Power*? This is about being proactive and on the offense. *It is far easier to create positive perception proactively then it is to replace a negative perception that is already in place.* Think about the laws of motion in physics, where an object in motion tends to stay in motion.

NOT AN EXACT SCIENCE

So, none of these numbers are an exact science. Rather, they are "rules-of-thumb" born out of experience, trial and error, and learning. They are guidelines that keep us on the playing field. The question can be, "How good can something be that is not exact?" Think no further than all the flights you may have taken on airlines. Believe it or not, aircraft design is not an exact science. Rather, it is based upon mathematical equations with end results rounded to the nearest tenth, hundredth, or even thousandth decimal point. Aircraft designs then undergo rigorous flight testing for design refinement, long before the mass production phase or a single passenger ever takes a seat on an airplane's maiden flight. Thus, our rule-of-thumb do not need to be exact sciences either. Rather, these rules similarly give leaders the capacity to have a relationship with the breadth and frequency needed for optimal communication and once there, leaders should assess and refine their approach as individual situations dictate.

STAY ON TOPIC AND BEWARE OF PRONOUNS

When sharing a perspective to manage perception, it is important to speak from identifying the viewing point of a position or decision. You might say, from the perceptive of managing all the players, that _____ is what is important, and from the perspective of being viable with this client in two years _____ is what is important. The issue here is that viewing points can be varied and a major caution is to avert instances in which there are only two perspectives where "My perspective is _____ while Joe's view is _____." This format makes the perspective personal and adds a layer of discourse into the conversation. In reality, there likely are multiple perspectives on any given topic, and a leader's goal must be, via *Perception Power*, to communicate their perspective while acknowledging those of other team members in such a way so that team cohesion is not impacted and the team remains viable.

TAKE THESE RULES-OF-THUMB, MAKE THEM YOURS AND ADD TO THEM

These rules-of-thumb are offered to give you some rules of thumb that have worked well over a period of years to champion perception power. They are not the only rules out there to be leveraged. Make these rules your own, by using them to champion your *Perception Power*. Along the way, you likely will discover some of your own rules and should you do so, please share them with me. Shoot me an email at linda@lindashaffer-vanaria.com

CALL TO ACTION

Your CALL TO ACTION with **SKILL TWO: Knowing and Leveraging the Numbers** is to explore/do the following:

1. Reflect on whether you leverage any numbers or Rules-of-Thumb in how you currently communicate. Note the

impacts of those numbers and Rules-of-Thumb on your PERCEPTION POWER.

2. Consider how being more deliberate with the 5 Rules-of-Thumb could enable you enhance your PERCEPTION POWER and increase your team's buy in, taking action and gaining momentum.

3. What practices will you start, continue or evolve to be more consistent with in knowing and leveraging the numbers to enhance your PERCEPTION POWER?

Chapter 4

SKILL THREE: Applying the Lesson of Pavlov's Dog

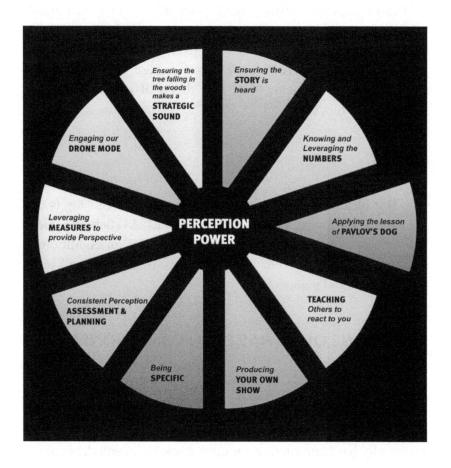

WHO WAS PAVLOV'S DOG?

Ivan Pavlov was a Russian scientist of the 1800's who studied conditioning. His test subjects were dogs and the dogs collectively are now referred to as "Pavlov's Dog." Immediately prior to feeding his dogs, Pavlov would ring a bell. Over time, Pavlov would ring the bell and the dogs would start salivating as they associated the bell with being fed. Pavlov had in fact conditioned his dogs to the sound of a bell. Our purpose here is to leverage this metaphoric concept of conditioning in how it relates to perception management. The point is that each one of us possess habits or thoughts that result from years of conditioning and if we want or need to recondition ourselves and others to think differently, we must engage our approach to perception management. Note that this will not be a snap of fingers and voila event.

BIG IDEA

The Big Idea here in applying the lesson of Pavlov's Dog is that we each have some of Pavlov's Dog inside us. As such, to achieve *Perception Power*, we must deliberately focus on conditioning our own preconceived responses to Pavlov's bell into transformational perspectives

EVERY ONE OF US HAS BEEN CONDITIONED

No matter how old we find ourselves, our habits and thoughts have largely been conditioned and cultivated for a number of years. In other words and in Pavlov's Dog terms, the bell repeatedly has been ringing for quite some time, and depending on the level of conditioning, sometimes longer than for others. Reconditioning, although difficult, can be powerful. It is about creating the capacity for reinventing and repurposing ourselves to meet the challenges we face, free from the barriers inherent to our previous perspectives and ways of working. The same is true for all the people we work with; even those who perpetually try new things. In terms of managing perception, this is about cultivating a new response. Knowing this upfront will aid us strategically to be deliberate, tenacious, and unrelenting in working to achieve such transitions and transformation. The whole thing here is that there is a transition process and ultimately a transformation, with the goal in Pavlovian terms being that although the bell may be ringing, the dogs are no longer salivating.

TAKING OWNERSHIP OF THE BELL

For our own habits and responses we own the bell. It is up to us to recondition our responses strategically to allow our perception to be influenced by others, while simultaneously facilitating others to be influenced by our perceptions. Some of you might be connoisseurs of antiques and restoring them or reworking them into new purposes that honor their origin. That is the essence of reconditioning. Here, we are transforming that piece to provide for something other than its original purpose. It increases the beauty of the piece, the desirability of the piece, and can create a whole audience who want it.

DELIBERATENESS AND PATIENCE

Transitions take being deliberate and patient. Sharing something with somebody who is not in the mood to hear it will be wasted time and may solicit a grimace. If you try again, this time you may solicit an outright snarl along with some form of recognition. The scenario may unfold something like "Hey, we've been doing this, and here's the results we're getting. Pretty exciting isn't it?" In this first exchange, the response may simply be "I don't see it." A few weeks later, you make a second attempt at sharing. This time, the response may be "Well, I'm starting to see where you're coming from, but I still don't like it." You persist in sharing and in your next attempt you get a "Well, I see where it's working. Wish it could be something different than that, but I think I understand why it needs to be." Here, with a bit of tenacity, you have reconditioned your colleague's response to the bell. It is important though to realize that everyone absorbs information, learns, and transforms at different rates and in different ways. I now have three dogs. They are all related yet they do not look like nor act alike. One practically potty-trained himself at 9 weeks old and after only a few trips outside. His brother was still on the potty-training program but improving after 8 years!

BEING AWARE OF OUR PAVLOV'S DOG MODE

One of my big lessons about what it means to add a little more of something to the equation came from learning to land high-performance jet aircraft on the aircraft carrier. In order to fly the airplane on glideslope to touchdown, smooth and subtle flight control inputs; power and stick must be made, while over-controlling the airplane will result in an erratic glidepath and missing the intended landing spot.

One of the most interesting insights that was shared with me by a seasoned pilot was that they simply thought about adding "just a small squeak extra power" to maintain glidepath. Anything more would cause the airplane either to "balloon" above glide path and miss the carrier's arresting wires, or too little to "settle" below glidepath into a very dangerous situation of crashing into the back of the ship. Managing our Pavlov's Dog mode is similar to landing on the ship in that we need to receive and offer small corrective inputs of reinforcement. Too much could push people away, while too little could cause a potentially disastrous result. In developing perception management skills, a calibrated sense of how to keep transitions and transformation moving forward will also be created. Being aware is the glide path to success!

LEVERAGING OUR SKILL OF KNOWING THE NUMBERS

With perception management, skills may stand on their own or potentially may be leveraged to build the impact of other skills. In reconditioning your own or others Pavlov's Dog Mode, leveraging the rules-of-thumb discussed previously will help in fostering more precise communication. Specifically, ensuring you have 7 - 12 touchpoints on the subject you wish to transition, presenting 4 - 8 perspectives to reduce resistance, and striving for 50 or more touchpoints to enable a long-term sustainability with ongoing revitalization every 4 - 6 weeks will be pivotal. This leverage can help you to condition the Pavlov's Dog Mode into a mode of reliability.

CALL TO ACTION

Your CALL TO ACTION with **SKILL THREE: Applying the Lesson of Pavlov's Dog** is to explore/do the following:

1. Reflect on how you have been conditioned with your communication and listening. Note what "The Bell" is ringing for and not ringing for.

2. Similarly reflect on how others around you, or your team, or your organization as a whole, has been conditioned with their communication and listening. Similarly note what "The Bell" is ringing for and not ringing for.
3. What supporting structures do you need to start, continue or evolve to be more consistent with enhancing how you apply the lesson of Pavlov's Dog in building your PERCEPTION POWER?

CHAPTER 5

SKILL FOUR: Teaching Others to React to You

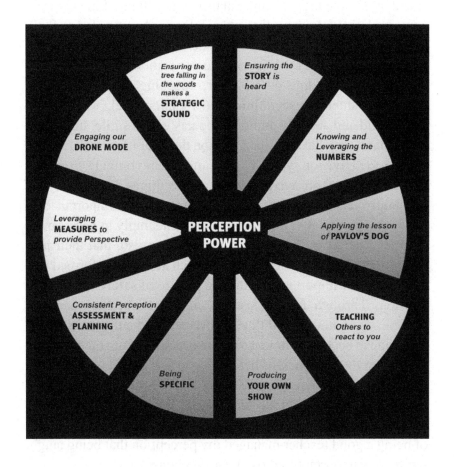

Over the years, one of the most common pieces of feedback I have received from those I have led is that I am a really good teacher. The first time I remember receiving this feedback was early in my first career as a Navy Pilot and from one of the enlisted personnel in my "ground job," as the Line Division Officer. In Navy squadron life, each pilot, in additional to their flight duties, is also assigned a "ground job," which, from day-to-day, you actually spend more time in performing than actually flying. Line Division personnel are the group that physically ready aircraft for flight and direct the aircraft's taxi from the flight line to the taxiway. Imagine yourself in a 1950s vintage gas station, with a swarm of attendants descending on your car; checking the oil, tires, fan belts, windshield washer fluid, and radiator level, washing the windshield and actually pumping the gas with a smile; that pretty much sums-up what the Line Division does for its aircraft. Sailors in the Line Division typically are quite young; ranging from 18 - 20 years of age on average. One of the things I found myself constantly teaching them was to understand the importance of their job; specifically, that they existed not simply to perform the services I detailed earlier, but rather, in doing so, that their jobs really were all about safety, and that each act they performed was one of utmost importance in the big picture of safely executing a mission. Through my consistent reinforcement, they came to recognize and understand this importance, and aura of discipline and pride in accomplishment came to permeate from the Division. Receiving the feedback of being a good teacher from one of my sailors, it triggered me to think about what I actually was teaching and why it was helpful, so that I could keep on reinforcing my message and perhaps even strengthen it. Receiving this feedback of being a good teacher managed my perception that being taught things was important to those I was leading.

BIG IDEA

The Big Idea, here with teaching others to react to you is that you cannot expect people to see through your eyes without a lens. So as leaders, we must give them the lens by teaching them how to see and understand your perspective and how it applies to them.

TEACHING BEGINS WITH UNDERSTANDING YOUR OWN REACTIONS

Even at the oddest of times, life has a way of teaching us key lessons, so long as one's eyes, ears, and mind are open to witness, process, and understand them. Early in my career as a Naval Aviator, I experienced an out-of-control flight emergency where in one instant, I was flying a high-performance jet airplane, and in the next, was snapped inverted, with the aircraft violently uncontrollable and plummeting out of the sky, with ground impact only seconds away. I initiated ejection via pulling the ejection handle, with the expectation that immediately, I would be rocketed out of the doomed airplane. That did not happen. Rather, the ejection seat malfunctioned and I found myself still trapped inside the airplane. I became more determined, holding my arm backwards to ensure that on my next attempt, I got the best possible pull on the ejection handle knowing that I only had time enough for one more try. As the seat shot-out, I ended up ripping my right shoulder out of its socket but had escaped what would have been certain death. I was rescued via helicopter, taken to the Naval Hospital, and admitted into the intensive care unit. But, I had survived!

At that time, I was the Navy's 9th woman jet pilot. Equally unusual was my nurse in the intensive care unit being a man, an event which has come to be common today. I do not know specifically how many men were nurses at that time, but can comment that he was the only one I ever met or knew in that role. He was a very dedicated nurse. While being treated by him, I remember thinking to myself, "a male nurse, how odd is that?" Then I immediately realized that he was taking care of a woman pilot and was likely also thinking to himself "a woman pilot, how odd is that?" Over the years, this encounter has stayed with me as a teaching moment and point of reflection. What I realized was in the moment that I met my nurse, I was making a judgement. I also realized that in that very same moment, the very person helping me also likely was making a judgement. What this taught me is that we all start with judgements of some kind and as a part of our basic survival and decision making. How I became different from that moment forward is in realizing that although people to have an inclination to initial judgement, that in teaching them and ultimately managing their perception, they can be taught to place that judgement aside and embrace other perceptions.

TEACHING BLOSSOMS FROM PERMISSION

What I have learned in my coaching practice is that giving permission for someone to arrive with whatever thoughts they have and to be themselves creates an environment where people can relax, feel safe, and be candid. It creates an environment where the focal point is not resistance but rather one of learning and transformation. Permission does not have to be formal as you might experience in the military with a verbal "permission granted." Rather, permission becomes a leader's style and actions. When offering perspectives and setting out to manage perceptions, we effectively are teaching others how to connect the dots that need to be connected. We are helping them to complete their picture of the world. To ensure we do not miss an

58

opportunity to evolve our own perspective and the perspective of others, we must, with some deliberateness, consciously set the tone through giving permission.

HOW THE LAW OF BEGETS TOUCHES TEACHING AND PERCEPTION

During a later tour as a Naval Aviator, I was an instructor in a Fighter Squadron, teaching out-of-control flight recovery techniques. At that time in the mid-1980s, the enticement of being a highly paid airline pilot was driving pilots to leave the Navy in large numbers. I remember our Wing Commander, a senior Navy Captain, coming to the squadron to speak to all the pilots to reinvigorate their passion for Naval Aviation. One of the things he said was "retention begets retention." He said this in such an intense and passioned way that I heard the echo of his deep voice saying this phrase over-and-over again in my head after he left. It was the word "begets" that drew my focus.

As I reflected on the word "begets," I realized that it can apply to just about everything. If someone comes into a room and they are angry, they do not need to make an announcement for everyone to be aware of their anger. Before you know it, the whole room is angry about something and they are not sure why. If someone walks into a room and is excited about something great that is happening, the conversation can readily be directed to great energizing things that are happening. Similarly, when we give permission, it begets others in giving us permission. When we teach, it begets others in teaching us. If we create pathways of managing perception, others will learn from those styles and pathways, returning their communication similarly. We thereby create flow and generate a cadence and momentum.

I once coached a particular client who was an absolutely diligent worker. He was continually handed more and more projects because of his unmatched competence. His boss was a quiet leader and operated with minimal communication. The perception the boss had exuded was that there was no permission to discuss priorities and reprioritization. My client, himself a leader, was getting so burned out that he simply wanted to leave. We talked about him giving himself permission to ask his boss for a routine 10-minute meeting, once every few weeks, to discuss work flow and prioritization. He asked for the meeting and the boss realized the need for more communication and started touching base periodically with him. The boss had seen my client as being so busy and diligent that his perception had been not interfere, as it might be a distraction. With my client making the first move of asking for something, it set the tone that his boss then readily gave himself permission to touch base without being an annoyance. Permission begot permission and new perceptions begot new perceptions. Both the boss and my client quickly came to alignment of priorities, and their newly found dialogue stimulated productivity. The questions for you here are what should you beget in enabling your work or perceptions to come to life and how will you begin the process so that the law of begets becomes your ally?

CALL TO ACTION

Your **CALL TO ACTION with SKILL FOUR: Teaching Others to React to You** is to explore/do the following:

1. Reflect on how you currently leverage the teaching of others on how to react to you and your team. Note the value of that teaching.

2. Reflect on the Law of Begets and how you can better leverage it in engendering enhanced PERCEPTION POWER to get your team to buy in, taking action and gain momentum.

3. What supporting structures do you need to start, continue or evolve to a new level of consistency with how you teach others to react to you, your team and your organization?

CHAPTER 6

SKILL FIVE: Producing Your Own Show

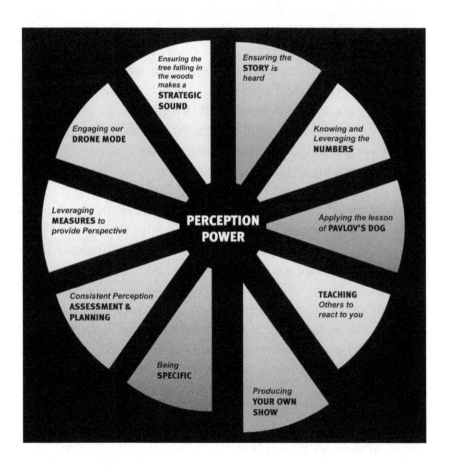

For as long as I can remember I have enjoyed a passion for cooking. As such, today, I watch many of the various cooking shows for entertainment as well as to learn new recipes and techniques. In viewing the recent trend of reality-based cooking shows, where contestants are engaged as team, a realization on perception management was triggered in me. I realized that these teams on cooking shows are like teams in businesses across a breadth of industries. They are teams on a mission to cook-up a winning result. In reflecting further through the lens of a cooking show, I realized that there are two essential types of characters which drive the customer to stay engaged; where the customer specifically is the wider television audience. These two types of characters are the contestant chefs themselves as well as the celebrity chef narrators. Quite often, the audience does not even see the narrators for extended periods of time; they may simply be a voice that highlights what is going on.

Cooking and the operational world of business are very much alike. In both, we use ingredients and processes to cook-up results. We may be cooking-up a great team attitude, a team capacity to innovate a solution, or a positive relationship with a potential customer. No matter, whatever we are cooking-up, as with any recipe, there will be special ingredients to be used and processes to be followed in order to achieve our desired results. Some of these ingredients and processes are directly tethered to bottom lines while some are tethered to the drivers; for example, a "positive relationship with a customer." Most operators do pretty well in completing their cooking challenge. The problem enters when others do not know or grasp the "who, whats, and whys" of their cooking efforts.

BIG IDEA

The Big Idea is that viewing perception management as producing your own cooking show will help you to direct your time, focus, and energy to manage and achieve the perceptions necessary for momentum in your unfolding success.

In coaching clients, I have noticed a common thread that leaders tend to make lists of things to be shared, missing the greater opportunity of managing perception. What has become clear to me is that leaders generally view the challenge of managing perception as one of sharing content and not from a perspective of producing a cooking show, requiring both contestants and narrators in becoming successful.

PRODUCING A SHOW BRINGS CLARITY TO THE ROLES REQUIRED

We all know that producers of shows do not spend extra time or money on characters they do not need. So why would producers spend money on celebrity chef narrators? What value do they serve? The answer to that question tells us the value of the narrator in producing perception.

The narrator is the one that tells you why the ingredient is the ingredient, what makes that ingredient special rather than ordinary, what makes the ingredient essential to the success of the meal, and in a contest, what makes a given chef or team of chefs destined to be the winner. The narrator also informs you of the process, why it is the process, why we should care about the process, and risks to the process, so as the audience we sit on the edge of our seats, wondering if the contestant chefs can pull it all off! The narrator, in other words, is the one that ensures that the show "speaks" to the audience and has meaning, engendering the audience's interest and a desire to come back for more shows. The narrator is the one who highlights the contestant chefs as anything from ordinary to innovator, with further characterization as expert, dedicated, masterful, and even hero thrown in for good measure (no pun intended. . .). Producers simply will not allow perceptions of attitude, skill, and success to be left to chance because if they did so, their ratings likely would plummet with their show eventually being cancelled.

When I share this metaphor with leaders whom I coach, I invite them to think of the frame of television being around their office or team. I invite them to think of themselves and their team as the contestants and celebrities of their own show. I ask them, what do they need others to know regarding what they are cooking and how they need the narration to flow in capturing the attention of their intended audience.

A GREAT VISIT DOES NOT NECESSARILY MAKE FOR A COMPLETE BIG PICTURE

Leaders who are great communicators and have a steady flow of communication in and out of their office, via email or on their walk to the parking lot, tend to think that if they have a few great conversations, then perception is well-managed. Let's again turn to the metaphor of our cooking show in analyzing this misconception. When people tune into a cooking show, they are seeing a snapshot in time. They do not understand the big picture of everything else that was going on before that snapshot or after they leave. When we have great connections it may seem logical to assume that a greater understanding of the big picture has transpired than in reality actually exists. It is really no different than the experience we get when channel surfing in looking for something interesting to watch. I remember channel surfing one day and seeing a clip for a movie in an advertisement. The movie's scene was particularly funny, so at my earliest opportunity, I went to see the full movie. Surprisingly, the movie was actually a tragedy with the clip I had seen being the only funny piece in the entire movie! Had I expected this I might not have been so disappointed but because I expected to see a comedy, henceforth, I would think twice before going to another movie based upon an advertisement or from that particular producer.

Producers create a picture through narration of a greater story which draws people in, and makes them want to stay and participate. When we do that as leaders, we are cooking-up the desire to participate and buy-in. By keeping people engaged, leaders openly invite and influence their realization of the need to take action. By keeping the show ongoing and building momentum, this occurs naturally. It is not about producing a long show; rather, it is about having a small amount of the right content from the right character. In reality, the leader may be taking on the roles of character and narrator. They need to do so with awareness and deliberateness or risk foiling the plot of their own story.

TAKE OWNERSHIP OF YOUR ROLES

Leaders today need to lead from more than one role. I see leaders in rapid growth, entrepreneurial businesses wearing lots of hats. Multiple roles may also happen in large corporations, but in entrepreneurial businesses, it is the norm for all leaders, generally speaking. What often happens is that the leaders latch onto their operational task roll. Accordingly, they set into a pattern of communicating their message on a specific task. If they are producing perception they would be clear on how many short shows they need to produce and what the contestant chef and celebrity chef narrator need to be doing and communicating in each show. They may need to provide separate time blocks to keep themselves focused and clear. For example, they may need to narrate what is happening in a given task and then separately, narrate what is occurring in the bigger picture as a Director, where the one task they just spoke about is only a small piece. If they miss producing either show, a disconnect will likely evolve which potentially will lead to a wider perception that the leader is not engaged in producing the right results in the right way.

LEARNING TO COOK FROM OTHERS

The opportunity is all around us, through studying best practices from others, and "upping our game" on how we cook and produce our own show. I personally have over 400 cookbooks that have come from travels, my family, and research where I sought them out. I similarly have a lot of leadership books too. Over the years, people ask, "What do you do with all those cookbooks?" Interestingly, I rarely follow a recipe exactly, but if I am going to make something new, I may pull-out four or five cookbooks; one, over a hundred years old, one, from a certain region, one, from a church, and perhaps one, from a collection of different family recipes. What this does is that it gets me prepared and forges a mindset, strategies, and options, so that I can actually start to cook, at which point I am not using a specific recipe at all. When we produce our own show, we similarly are creating the awareness that we are there doing whatever we are doing however we are doing it, such that others can reach out to us strategically and specifically. The shows we produce enlighten our meaning to others so that others see us in the context of whatever they are doing as well. In that way, everyone can keep cooking-up the solutions that are in alignment with their needs.

Now it is your time to name the show or shows that you are producing or need to produce and I wish you great productions and perception ratings!!!

CALL TO ACTION

Your CALL TO ACTION with **SKILL FIVE: Producing Your Own Show** is to explore/do the following:

1. Reflect on the show your producing now. What do your "ratings" tell you regarding your PERCEPTION POWER? Or regarding the PERCEPTION POWER of your team?
2. Reflect about the different shows you need to produce and whether they each get the dedication they need to exude PERCEPTION POWER?
3. What supporting structures do you need to start, continue or evolve to have greater consistency to ensure your own show or shows get your team or organization to buy in, take action and gain momentum?

CHAPTER 7

SKILL SIX: Being Specific

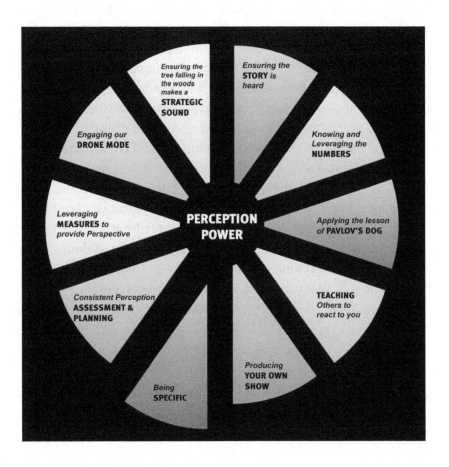

There is a common tendency in leaders to believe that in asking questions that are broad or general in nature, that they are opening a door with their people for open and honest communication. In reality, it does not work that way. In attempting to open the door of communication, leaders typically ask something very general, such as "How is everything going?" So general a question actually does not spurn communication, rather, it stifles it. Let me explain. The way that "How is everything going?" typically is answered is that the question's recipient will either think "Is there a problem," or "Does he or she think there's a problem," or "I'd better quickly figure out what the problem is that he or she wants to know about." Here, immediately, the question's recipient has been put into a defensive posture and any hope for meaningful open communication has been lost. At best, the leader will get a response something like "All good," or "Everything's great," with the question's recipient thinking that "He or she really doesn't want to know how it's going, they're just making small-talk." Even should the leader get a little more specific with something like "I'm working on my communication, how am I doing," the recipient likely will offer something similar to the earlier response, such as "You're doing great, keep doing what you're doing" This kind of feedback may be friendly and cordial, but not helpful in raising the bar or managing perception and ideas in moving forward.

BIG IDEA

The Big Idea here with being specific is that to manage perception with decisiveness, you must endeavor deliberately to be specific.

BEING SPECIFIC IS MORE THAN SIMPLY ADDING A FEW KEY SPECIFICS

The intention of being specific is to ensure that your message is received in such a way there is no ambiguity or room for an alternative understanding. During our discussion on the skill of ensuring your story is heard, we talked about the distinction between details and key specifics. Here, we are talking about refining your approach on being specific, so that it becomes a true instrument of decisiveness creation and shared understanding.

When we are specific, we might share something such as, "I have been working on setting a new tone in how our meetings are getting started. Specifically, I have been trying to start with the big picture, to share something that is uniquely significant about what each person has been doing toward the strategy, and then moving from there into talking about some of the challenges we are facing and how to solve them. How is this working for you? What else can take it to the next level?" Here, you are sharing key specifics to manage perception around what is occurring, along with the intentions and other elements that paint a picture. This now sets the stage for the person or group hearing your message to react spontaneously and honestly.

SETTING YOUR FULCRUM ON YOUR LEVEL OF SPECIFICITY

From the time I was four years old through my high school years, I was a springboard diver. One of the first things an experienced springboard diver does before mounting the board is to set the fulcrum. This adjusts the amount of spring in the board. When that adjustment is fine-tuned, the diver's expectation is that he or she will have just the right amount of spring and control for the dive. Typically, the fulcrum will be set differently, depending on the dive to be attempted, for each of their dives. Similarly, when being specific in our communication, we serve as the fulcrum, ensuring our message is focused and understood with precision and clarity. Here, we must realize that depending upon the situation, being specific will require a range of detail; sometimes, just a little, and other times, a lot of detail will be required. The key question to be asked here is "What is the right amount of detail needed to engender perception in the way it needs and must be?"

THE NEED FOR DEFINING KEY ELEMENTS

In communication, our tendency is to assume that language we have heard before carries the same meaning with everyone. For example, if a leader remarks "Let's work extra hard on being a team," we might assume that everyone knows what it means to be a team and holds the same perception on the need and value of having a team to tackle the project being discussed. One of my clients once remarked that they "want their team to be more 'teamy.'" I asked "How would you know a 'teamy' team if you saw one?" "What would make you say, that is the most 'teamy' team I ever saw?" My client then shared a litany of key elements that were needed to achieve being "teamy." Thus, being "teamy' was defined. When we define key elements, we specifically set our fulcrum in ensuring people's perceptions are aligned to our own. We also must understand that precision here is based on clarity and that absent clarity, the leader's key elements and those of his or her team will certainly differ.

BEING SPECIFIC WITH ACKNOWLEDGEMENTS

Significant in being specific and championing perception management is deliberate acknowledgement. Acknowledgement is beyond saying "good job." Such a comment is really more of a complement rather than a full-out acknowledgement of someone's accomplishment. When we acknowledge, we share the details of what is occurring; how behavior and processes are manifesting specific outcomes. We also share the specific qualities of the person or team that enabled this outcome. You might share something like "You've been managing several projects and the difficulty there is in keeping so many critical balls in the air. I want to take a moment to share the exceptional impact of your approach to _____, which enabled all of us to stay ahead of the game."

You might then champion their perception of how their accomplishment fits into the unfolding story of a next success by saying "We have a huge challenge facing us in the week ahead. The same approach you took with _____ can be applied to _____ in meeting this challenge." Thus, in championing, you are managing their own perceptions of their value in creating a specific outcome. When we become mindful of acknowledgement, we have the opportunity to think about what perspectives would be wise to acknowledge so others feel heard and understood. Before closing here, one cautionary word on acknowledgement, *It must be timely.* During my Naval career, I unfortunately witnessed, time-after-time, superior performers being acknowledged for accomplishments that were months or even years ago. How de-motivating it is for someone to be recognized for something that now, no longer is relevant or at best, is stale? My advice here is that if a leader believes an accomplishment is important enough to warrant acknowledgement, *then it is also important enough for timely acknowledgement.*

CALL TO ACTION

Your CALL TO ACTION with **SKILL SIX: Being Specific** is to explore/do the following:

1. Reflect on the details in your communication; specifically, "How many of the details in your communication are simply detail?" and, "How many of the details are "Key Specifics?""
2. Reflect on what "Key Specifics" you tend to leave out of your communication and the impact that leaving them out may have on your PERCEPTION POWER.
3. What terms or elements in your approaches or communication would benefit from being specifically defined to garner the "Key Specifics?" How would defining these elements enhance your PERCEPTION POWER and get your team or organization to buy in, take action and gain momentum?

CHAPTER 8

SKILL SEVEN: Consistent Perception Assessment & Planning

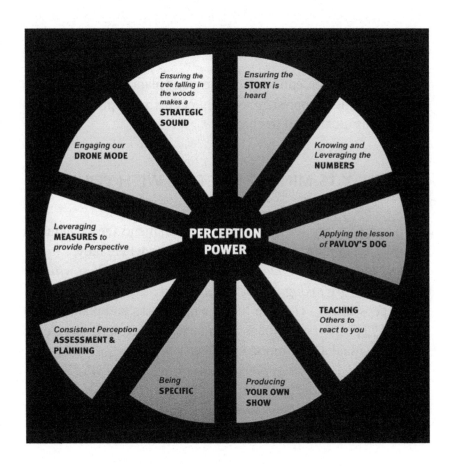

Perception is something that leaders generally care about. That said, a common thread I observe in my coaching practice is that only a handful of leaders employ consistent approaches in assessing and planning how they manage perception. Assessment and planning are parts of managing anything well. So, to become masterful, the skills of assessment and planning must become a part of your perception management process.

BIG IDEA

The Big Idea in perception assessment and planning is that leaders must own their approach to architecting perceptions so that perceptions are not left to chance.

MONTHLY 15-MINUTE MEETING WITH YOURSELF

With nearly every leader I coach, I recommend they conduct a monthly 15-minute meeting with themselves where they:
Update their Evolving Development Goals Action Plan with the actions they are taking and next plan to take.
This keeps leaders clear on their own progress and plan, so that their key specifics will focus and manage perceptions regarding their individual and corporate results.
Review what perceptions they need to foster; specifically, how do they need and want their stakeholders to think, feel, and act regarding their development areas or for that matter, anything else?

Most leaders initially consider someone feeling something as "touchy-feely soft stuff." The truth is that identifying what you need someone to feel in order to ensure buy-in or take action is truly strategic. You might need someone to feel that their skills are uniquely significant. You might need them to feel that it is now or never and that you really need their support. In employing this type of granularity in identifying how you need your stakeholders to feel, you must first determine what it is that you need to share with them in order to elicit your desired response. You must communicate succinctly on what you need your stakeholders to understand. As such, you are enabling the start of dialogue between your stakeholders and yourself regrading what you and they need from each other. There is an old leadership expression that "structure drives behavior." How someone thinks or feels is a structure for how they will act. Similarly, when you consider the specific things that you want or need your stakeholders to be thinking, it enables you to be clear on how you must manage their perceptions.

So, in your 15-minute meeting, check in with yourself on what you believe you have communicated to others over the past month. If you have ensured some communications occurred, it may be your prompt to reinvigorate them with a fresh mention. If you have not shared anything that connects those dots you need connected, then you can take for action to close the loop in communicating those things in the week ahead. This keeps your perception management flowing with our previously discussed rule-of-thumb for communication every 4 to 6 weeks.

Before closing this section, the story of a client from years back comes to mind. He expressed that a mismatch existed; between his belief of what was going on in his team and how his team perceived him. At the time we started with coaching, he had not even thought about perception management. I asked him, "What is your approach to ensure your people and you are on the same page? He replied, "I believe that my world is the way that I see it." We worked on him engaging in dialogue with his people and in doing so, what it is that he needed his people to perceive. He was shocked at the renewed commitment and engagement of his people. His mastering of the 15-minute meeting became an ongoing part of his approach to leadership thereafter.

Now, imagine if you took full ownership of managing your people's perceptions. What are some of the things that people around you might be thinking, feeling, or taking action upon that could be enhanced from what they are doing right now? How significant could that be toward engendering buy-in and momentum?

TAKING A STRATEGIC PAUSE

In working day-to-day, most of us at some point will receive emergent tasking or encounter pop-up situations where managing perceptions will be crucial. Simply taking a short strategic pause of a few minutes to ask yourself some questions or leverage a focusing process you created will enable you better to assess the situation and what must be communicated, how you must communicate, and the timeframe you have to enact your communication. Such a pause may be appropriate for as little as 30 seconds before walking into a meeting, to become clear on the top two things you need to ensure those in the meeting think and feel prior to leaving the room. In sharing this concept with a client, he went from being someone who listens and reflects in meetings to one who is engaged. Perceptions of others went from viewing him as an operational asset to where they now viewed him as a strategic player.

For those is large global organizations, where you are entering a meeting with leaders you infrequently communicate with, you might pause before the meeting and ask yourself, "What do I need them to think and feel about my engagement, during the meeting and thereafter, to show that I care about working with them?" In my Navy career, the term here was "interoperability;" an ability to work together between different service branches (Navy, Army, Air Force, Marines) and even different coalition partner nations as well. I now am starting to hear the term interoperability also being used in the private sector! By adding a sprinkle of this content into the conversation, it can manage the perception that you are a big-picture thinker and a global team player. This is all about small shifts of content for rather large strategic perception shifts and I hope you are seeing the power of a 30 second strategic pause.

SHOOTING FROM A STRATEGIC HIP

In a very - very busy disruptive world, strategic pauses and short meetings can feel like something that is extra rather than the strategic event it is. When you take this time, you are effectively setting yourself up to be spontaneous in the perception management of your daily communications. Most leaders have impromptu meetings with people during their day, where they bump into someone in a hallway, have an unexpected call, or participate in a pop-up. When we leverage our 15-minute assessment, planning meetings, and strategic pauses, our thoughts are clear on what is essential to manage perceptions. We have all heard the expression about shooting from the hip. Typically, shooting from the hip is considered somewhat reckless or haphazard. Yet when we come to impromptu situations with insights based upon our 15-minute meetings and strategic pauses, it will enable the hips we are shooting from to be ready strategically to manage perceptions. When this is the case, you are shooting from a "strategic hip."

CALL TO ACTION

Your CALL TO ACTION with **SKILL SEVEN: Consistent Perception Assessment & Planning** is to explore/do the following:

1. Reflect on whether the impromptu communications of yourself, your team and your organization are supported with a "Strategic Hip."
2. Reflect on how a monthly 15-Minute Meeting could support you with building your PERCEPTION POWER. Take action on starting your monthly 15-Minute Meeting if you currently do not have one on your calendar.
3. Reflect on how you can leverage the Strategic Pause to grow your PERCEPTION POWER to the next level.
4. What supporting structures do you need to start, continue or evolve to enable consistent perception assessment and planning that builds your PERCEPTION POWER?

Chapter 9

SKILL EIGHT: Leveraging Measures to Provide Perspective

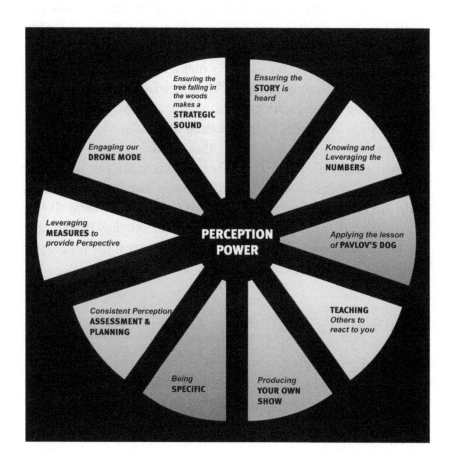

There is an expression that "What gets measured, gets done, and what gets noticed, gets repeated." In coaching leaders, an observation I have had is that leaders feel significantly busier now than they did just a few years ago. Organizations have leaned themselves with supposed process streamlining and thereby reducing people, or presenting more work to their people in the spirit of maximizing outcomes and opportunities. With such a phenomenon in play, I hear from clients all-the-time that they come to work with an approach of rolling-up their sleeves and getting to their work, sometimes even bypassing a cup of coffee. My term for them here is "going linear," where they remark "I can only do so much," and so, they make a list and start checking things off as they complete them. This approach ultimately misses the mark on opportunities to be more strategic, create better prioritization, and more ease in scaling of efforts. The perception they project to the world in this mode is that they are overwhelmed with all on their plate and struggling to keep their head above water. This perception may in fact hold them back from the promotion they want and are potentially a great fit for. It may bring them to a point where they feel like they need a new job to get away and have a fresh start, whereupon the process of building to the same crescendo starts all over again.

BIG IDEA

The Big Idea of leveraging measures to provide perspective is that in order to appreciate the significance of where we are and where we are heading, we need a measurable reference point.

CREATING MEASURES FOR THE SEEMINGLY NON-MEASURABLE

Where I came to appreciating measures in bringing clarity to what could otherwise be branded as ambiguous, was as a test pilot. There, I gained respect for creating measures for the seemingly non-measurable, a skill that is becoming essential is today's fast-paced world. At that time, aircraft ergonomic design was shifting largely from analog style gauges and flight control systems to "fly-by-wire," which refer to computer driven displays and interfaces. This was a huge change and necessitated a complete re-write of the manner in which flight tests were performed and results judged against the specifications to which the aircraft was designed. It required a whole different way of communicating why something was or was not the way that it needed to be. This is what taught me the power of relative measures in communicating an impact and I have come to realize it as an essential skill of communication.

What you are enabling by bringing measures to the otherwise ambiguous is the capacity to showcase your situation in such a way that you can get the feedback needed for your next choices and decisions. You will also enable the capacity for people to see where they are at, their impact, and how they can emerge into their next impacts. It helps people to understand that what they are doing is valuable, how it is valuable, how it will be valuable next, and how to share with others how the value path and value proposition of their efforts are being created.

A STORY FROM IMPLEMENTING CHANGE IN MY SQUADRON

When I was a squadron commander, we engaged in a large transformation to move from our aircraft being shore-based to being embarked on the aircraft carrier 24/7 as a ready asset, at the snap of a finger. This transformation required huge cultural change and also a lot of major operational changes in working with the aircraft carrier and its supporting entities. In a bigger picture, it also involved manpower reviews and operationally rewriting how to do what we needed to do. The amount of change necessary here created an environment of working in my current role as well as adding to it an extra role in innovating the new way of working, which felt like a full-time job in its own right. What I could see is that there was so much happening and that still needed to be done, that people were getting lost in measuring their place in and contribution to the process. In implementing measures into our dialogue, it helped me to champion my people in seeing their story of unfolding results and also provided the capacity for me specifically to acknowledge the actions and contributions of key individuals in creating those impacts. When this dialogue and championing occurred, I saw a heightened sense of purpose, enthusiasm, and energy. It was a valuable lesson for me in seeing the incredible impact of an organization in transformation, in how measures connect to dialogue, which connect to buy in, which connects to momentum; all of which connect to the ultimate impact of well managed perception.

MEASURES TO SHOWCASE EMERGENCE AND TURNAROUND

From the outside looking in, if a leader is working on turning-around an organization or team that is in rough condition, I have heard people say "Well, it's really easy to shine in a place like that!" The truth is that "shining" only will occur if the leader communicates the evolving turnaround effectively. Why that is the case is that we tend to benchmark whether we are doing things appropriately from what is ideal. If it is not what we want, then we tend to judge something as bad or ineffective; rather than "formally horrendous and on the path to highly effective." When we paint the picture with the verbiage of the latter; the story of unfolding transformation, we command a perception of respect and a reputation as a leader who can turn things around!

You may be that leader that is turning things around but to have people see it, requires communication in parallel to manage perception. Leveraging measures is critical for leaders to showcase how their success is unfolding. An example of using such measures might be "We are moving forward with swiftness here. Specifically, on a scale from 1 to 10, where a '1' stands for being reactionary with things not aligned to the customer and a '10' stands for being proactive with things totally aligned, last month, we started at a '2' and already, we are up to a '7.' What specifically made it a 2 was _____. Via shifting our team meetings approach and daily check-in practices via _____ we moved that number to a '7'. Now, let's focus on moving it even higher, and the support I'll need from you to make that happen is_____."

Such communication tethers every observation and action taken to a measured impact. It showcases the turnaround via descriptions of experiences occurring linked to a measure of the impact it is, will be, and should be having in the future. As such, it enables the "soft" information you are noticing to impart a "hard" impact, with connection to bottom line results, leadership expectations, and also strategic measures. When we communicate this way, we leverage measures and inject them in the skill of ensuring our story is heard. This is the essence of a high-impact communication approach and not a dry exercise. It can change the feedback you receive from "I need you to tell me what is happening because I am concerned about_____ ," to "Wow, you really have a grip around this. This is very powerful, I can see how you are creating this transformation. Thanks for letting me know how I can help."

This communication of including measures can be relatively simple. You can create the measure readily in the context of any conversation once you understand how. You can also leverage using the same measures over again where your consistency with that measure enables showcasing evolution and growth. You simply are making it easier for your audience to understand why the things you are telling them are important, why they are key specifics and not details, and where things are expected to go next.

CONNECTION OF MEASURES TO ADOPTION

Globally, there is a shift to bring technology into business. There are accordingly shifts in what is being accomplished via technology and what is being accomplished via human interface. This is a huge cultural shift and also requires innovation in business practices to enable *Adoption*.

The real topic here is about bringing measurements to ambiguous situations and environments in such a way that people will reflect, "I see where you're at, I see what's moving forward and I see how I fit into the equation with an opportunity to solve challenges." In working with leaders and organizations focused on *Adoption*, they are working in environments where emotions often include fear and uncertainty, which engenders resistance. They need measures to help champion perceptions, alleviate fear, and have people see their self-value in the unfolding story of creating impact. It is a clear application for showcasing emergence and turnaround as we discussed earlier.

BEING DELIBERATE WITH HOW YOU LEVERAGE MEASURES

Now you are seeing the power that measures can have in showcasing your results, championing others, and managing perceptions. The question is now "How will you choose to be more deliberate with how you leverage measures?" Your goal is to use measures on a regular basis in such a way that you are bringing people to an understanding of how to address challenges, help be part of the solution, and ultimately understand your appreciation for their contribution to the results being witnessed.

Measures in this way provide an incredible opportunity to influence buy-in, taking action, and engendering momentum.

CALL TO ACTION

Your CALL TO ACTION with **SKILL EIGHT: Leveraging Measures to Provide Perspective** is to explore/do the following:

1. Reflect on the opportunities you have to create measures for the seemingly non-measurable.
2. Reflect on how you can become more deliberate in leveraging measures to showcase your turnarounds and unfolding success to get your team or organization to buy in, take action and gain momentum.
3. What supporting structures do you need to start, continue or evolve to have greater consistency to support your leveraging measures to provide perspective and enhance your PERCEPTION POWER?

CHAPTER 10

SKILL NINE: Engaging Our Drone Mode

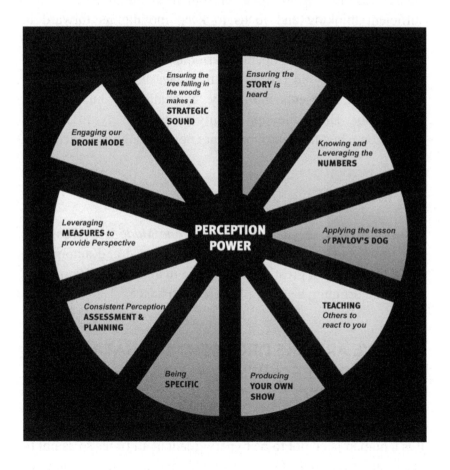

In movies and in some video games today, there are character drones, clones, and other forms of beings that operate with what is deemed a lower level of consciousness. One of my realizations in watching these movies and characters is that, in truth, we all have a mode that operates like that. It is not insulting ourselves, but rather, a simple acknowledgment that we cannot be hypervigilant every moment of each day. Continuous hypervigilance would be too hard on our bodies as there would be no time for rejuvenation. We are talking about a mode where we put less thinking and focus on something but in general, have sufficient thinking and focus to keep moving us forward in nominal ways. I have come to call this mode our *Drone Mode*. Knowing that all of us operate periodically in that mode, where we may not fully absorb all the messages in a situation or the environment, presents not only a challenge, but also an opportunity. Here, the opportunity is proactively to manage perception when those around us are not offering resistance.

BIG IDEA

The Big Idea on engaging those in *Drone Mode* is to recognize that people operate within a range of vigilance and automation and that we have a great opportunity to manage perception when others are droning; a state of lowered resistance.

HOW WE ARE LIKE DRONES AND WHAT THAT MEANS FOR PERCEPTION MANAGEMENT OPPORTUNITY

It is a human need not to be hypervigilant at all times so as not to burn ourselves out. Our *Drone Mode*, or reduced state of vigilance, is the body's physical approach to that. So, when you are thinking about engaging someone's *Drone Mode*, you need to ask yourself "What is the message I want to plant that fully takes advantage of their *Drone Mode*?" When you plant a message then, you can water it until it grows into a flower or whatever you need it to be.

To illustrate what we mean by *Drone Mode*, you may share "We are working on ____ and we are all incredibly excited about the _____ results. What is so exciting about the results is_____. We are looking at sustaining these results by____ and making them even more exciting by_____." Normally, the above likely would solicit comment and even argument on its finer points from an engaged audience. But. . . when in a *Drone Mode*, the way this may be heard and absorbed is "_____ is doing some very exciting things that are taking ____ and the whole organization to the next level." They may not fully remember everything but they remember the message's essence and put it into memory without analysis. This is an opportune time to plant messages that need to be heard without risk of debate.

When sharing to people in *Drone Mode,* they tend to remember the larger message along with the emotion and intention in which it was presented. The significance here is that if emotion and intention are not shared, people will tend to fill them in with something less aligned, less positive, and often negative. Think about what this could mean over a year of communication. Think of all the opportunities you have to plant messages that you can water without resistance. Think about what it could be like to have hundreds or thousands of messages that generate a spirit of excitement and alignment. What could that do for you? What could that do for your work life? What could that do for creating buy-in, taking action, and gaining momentum?

BE ALERT THAT DRONE MODE IS DISTINCT FROM AUTO-PILOT MODE

We have all had experiences where we have driven to or home from work, and when you get there, you barely have any recollection of the drive itself. When you realize this, it can be a frightening experience. You might ask yourself "How did I get here safely?" What just transpired here on the drive to and from work is what I call *Autopilot Mode*. *Autopilot Mode* stems from familiarity and repetition such that our minds "Tune-out" the task we are performing, since we have completed this exact same task over, and over, again. Instead of just driving home, what if somebody remarked, "Hey, on your way home today, take a look at_____, the progress they've made there is really amazing." Here, you likely would be alert to notice and pay attention to whatever it was that had been highlighted so that you could comment about it, when next you connect. Effectively, here, you have pulled out of *Autopilot Mode*, because your familiarity and repetition of your drive is being broken by the "whatever" it is you are supposed to look at. This is different from the *Drone Mode,* where you are not doing exactly the same thing that you do every day (such as drive home) but you are engaged in tasks that you deem unworthy or unnecessary of your strictest attention. The point to *Drone Mode* is that engagement with others is occurring, albeit it at a very reduced state and therefore, due to this reduced state, opportunity exists more easily to plant seeds.

CALL TO ACTION

Your CALL TO ACTION with **SKILL NINE: Engaging Our Drone Mode** is to explore/do the following:

1. Reflect on the difference between our Drone Mode and Autopilot Mode and how each manifests in your day-to-day and emergent operations.

2. Reflect on opportunities you have to leverage the Drone Mode in your communications, and how to leverage the numbers and Rules-of-Thumb from SKILL TWO as well as the other PERCEPTION POWER skills you have learned and been mastering.

5. What supporting structures do you need to start, continue or evolve in order to enable you to consistently leverage others' Drone Mode in building PERCEPTION POWER for you, your team, or your organization?

CHAPTER 11

SKILL TEN: Ensuring the Tree Falling in the Woods Makes a Strategic Sound

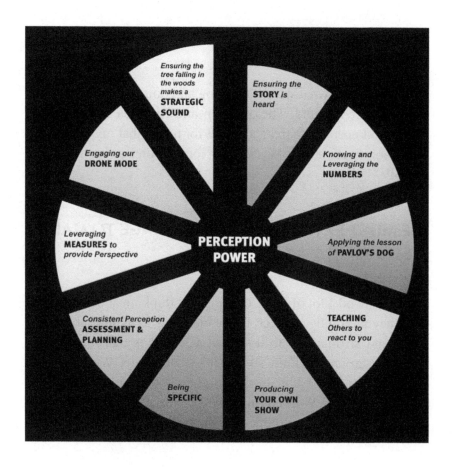

Most everyone has heard the age-old adage of the tree falling in the woods and the question that goes with it "Does it make a sound?" If you have to ask whether something is making a sound with your communication, then you are not being effective enough. As the facilitator for an intervention engagement some years ago, the purpose was to focus leadership on strategy, values, and alignment. At one point, a few of the senior leaders there were joking around and playing a game on whether or not they knew their company's four values. "Well, I guess we know two out of four," I heard. If these four values had been trees if the woods, only two of four would have fallen with a sound!

BIG IDEA

When we share what we are thinking and doing, the trees that are falling make a sound. The question and Big Idea then is "What sound do I need these trees to make for me so that my message is being communicated?" We are then focused on making a strategic sound!

WE MUST EXTROVERT OUR MESSAGE TO MAKE A SOUND

Leaders spend a lot of time focusing and thinking about whatever it is they are doing. In fact, the tendency is to assume that since we spend so much time doing whatever it is that we do, that everyone around us knows what it is that we do. We likely feel that way because what we do dominates our entire day, week, month, and year. We naturally get to a place where do not even consider that those around us may in fact not know what we are

doing! So, when we think and do things, trees actually may be
falling in the woods!!!

LESSONS FROM REDWOOD TREES

Metaphorically, when I think of trees falling in the woods and
making a sound, I often think of the redwoods. In the redwood
forest, you see many trees that have fallen. A redwood forest is
like no other; there is such density to these trees that the forests
are eternally in shadow, yet they flourish in spite of the limited
light which reaches ground level. Interestingly, the root structure
of redwoods is really quite shallow, pausing us to consider "How
can such tall trees stand with such shallow roots?" The answer is
that redwoods' roots are heavily intertwined. So, if one of the
redwood trees falls over, it may actually continue to grow. It
makes its sound via connecting the roots. So, thinking about the
redwoods, what kind of root structures do you have in terms of
how you send your thoughts, profile your actions, and
connections to others?" When we think this way and like the
redwoods, even if a tree is not able to stand on its own, it is
supported and sustained.

A NAVY STORY ABOUT STARTING AN
ORGANIZATION IN JAPAN

While a Department Head in a Navy squadron located in San
Diego, I was selected to stand-up a detachment; a small
component of a squadron. Unlike this squadron's four other
detachments which also were located in San Diego, my

detachment; Detachment Five, would be located in Japan. Upon arrival there, I found myself in a situation similar to what most managers from time-to-time in business face; not enough time ideally to ready the detachment for sustained flight operations and without the full complement of people I was supposed to have to make that happen!

Intent on performing my mission, I did not want to complain about the situation, yet it was my responsibility to ensure that the trees falling in the woods here made a strategic sound. The conversation with my supervisor, the Air Wing Commander (known as CAG, which actually stands for Carrier Air Group; a hold-over term from back when Air Wings were still called Air Groups) went something like "CAG, I'd like to tell you that I am doing _____," thereby acknowledging that I knew ideally what should be done. But, then I added, "Here is what is going to happen instead." To which I added, "We are going to marginally pass our _____ inspection but we will pass by doing it with our _____ plan so you can count on us be operational by _____." To which I then added "Making this is going to require all-hands working 12 on and 12 off. It would really mean a lot if you could come and cheer everyone on." I remember the CAG reacting like snapping out of fog, with a realization and then saying "yes, that's amazing." I realized from his reaction that if I had not managed his perception around the trees falling in the woods to make a strategic sound, that I probably would have been in his office, standing at attention and explaining myself, after marginally passing that inspection. That was a real lesson to me and is one of those situations that over the years, I still think about. It mentored me to consider "How must I manage the trees in my midst to make a strategic sound?"

CALL TO ACTION

Your CALL TO ACTION with **SKILL TEN: Ensuring the
Tree Falling in the Woods Makes a Strategic Sound** is to
explore/do the following:

1. Reflect on all the different "trees" that you have in your
   "woods." Note which ones make the biggest sound and
   why; and which ones make little to no sound and why.
2. Reflect on which "trees" you tend to extravert and which
   ones you tend to introvert. What is the impact of each on
   your PERCEPTION POWER?
3. Reflect on the lessons from Redwood Trees and how they
   apply to you on building your Strategic Sounds; specifically,
   with the inter-dependencies between yourself, your team and
   your organization.
4. What supporting structures do you need to start, continue or
   evolve to be more consistent with how you make your
   sounds Strategic Sounds?

CONCLUSION

"Perception is never final."

Linda Shaffer-Vanaria

TAKING OWNERSHIP OF YOUR PERCEPTION POWER

You have now been provided 10 proven skills employed by leaders in enabling their teams to buy-in, take action, and gain momentum. Knowing these skills is not enough. As leaders, we all know that success comes from leveraging and using what we have learned. As you finish reading this book and as your final key take-away, you must remember that *Perception is never final.* Accordingly, via the skills you now have, you continually must ensure that the perceptions of your team, department, division, or corporation are aligned to those of your own and both are in fact the way that you want or need them to be.

The pace of today's business world is fast and filled with distractions. The never-ending process of optimizing your success and as a by-product, making your life as smooth as possible, mandates taking ownership of perception management in your operational and strategic leadership realms. To do that with decisiveness is to give yourself and team the gift of *PERCEPTION POWER.*

Now the question to you is "How will you ensure that you take ownership of your *PERCEPTION POWER?*

PERCEPTION POWER MASTERY

As you reap the benefits of these skills in building your *PERCEPTION POWER*, many of you will want to grow your *PERCEPTION POWER* mastery to the next level. Because *PERCEPTION POWER*, in engendering buy-in, taking action, and gaining momentum, is such a key ingredient to success in leadership today, I am offering programs as well as coaching initiatives to take your mastery to the next level. Programs include master classes with strategies to build capacity in leveraging these skills, while coaching will provide tailored approaches not only to the complexities and challenges you face but also to the opportunities, known and yet to be discovered, to which you are or soon will be positioned. Programs will be featured at: www.lindashaffer-vanaria.com. Please join our mailing list at https://www.lindashaffer-vanaria.com/ or reach out to Linda directly at Linda@LindaShaffer-Vanaria.com.

APPENDIX: INTERVIEWS

INTERVIEW: Maya Hu-Chan Insights on Perception in Global and Cross-Cultural Leadership

I met Maya Hu-Chan over 10 years ago as part of a global consortium of colleagues called Alexcel Group. We have connected periodically to swap perspectives over the years and I have always had a deep regard for Maya's expertise with Global Leadership and Cross-Cultural Leadership. In the latter part of my writing my book, Maya and I had connected for lunch to catch up on all we each have been doing. I asked her for the opportunity to interview her to provide the readers of PERCEPTION POWER with practical insights on perception with global and cross-cultural leadership and also for her to share her perspectives on the value of some of the skills in PERCEPTION POWER in enabling buy in, taking action and gaining momentum. She speaks to the need for meaningful conversations. These interviews come in this book as an Appendix following the presentation of "What is Perception?" and, the 10 Skills for building your Perception Power so that you will have those elements and skills as building blocks to which you can augment with insights from the experts interviewed.

Note that the interview has been edited.

Linda: Thank you for taking time out today to give you views on perception and add practical insight to the skills in PERCEPTION POWER. I know we have known each other for many years, but why don't you describe to the audience who you are in a few words, so they can really understand your background. Please tell the reader a little bit about yourself.

Maya: Sure, thank you Linda. I appreciate the opportunity for this interview and to share my thoughts and insights about perceptions. I am an executive coach, speaker, author, and a leadership consultant. I have been doing this for over 20 years, and I work with mostly global leaders around the world and major corporations. The topics I focus on are mainly related to cross-culture leadership and also global leadership. I am an author and have actually co-authored and authored a total 11 books. I am also an economist, writing columns regularly for major publications such as Inc.com. Also, I am from Taiwan originally and I live in the U.S.A.

Linda: Great, and so you have this global perspective and the topic is perception power. I have shared with you about my book here on the 10 skills of Perception Power and their intention of enhancing team buy-in, taking action and gaining momentum through managing perception with leveraging those skills. In your view, how significant is perception in the equation of success of generating significant positive momentum in global leadership?

Maya: Well, I think we often say perception equals reality. That definitely has a lot of truth to it, but based on my experience working with leaders around the world, I also think that perception is closely linked to assumptions. For example with employees, there are employees who think that, "Well, if I do a good job, my boss will notice and promote me." That is the assumption based on this employee's background, experience, and culture. Their perception is "If I do a good job, my boss will know it and they will promote me or he will promote me. So, I do not need to tell him or her about what I have done, my accomplishment as it is bragging."

Linda: You have done a lot of work with China and other parts of the world. How has that shifted your view on managing perception?

Maya: A lot of the employees or professionals who are working, say, in Asia or in Latin America, often they will make that assumption that, "My work is going to speak for itself." They have that assumption, and it actually becomes part of their belief. Then that assumption can create a wrong perception in the manager's part. If they have a manager that is with a different background, say, from the U.S.A or from Canada or from Germany; they may think, "Well, this employee seems to be doing a good job, but he rarely speaks up at meetings, he does not really tell me what he has done or what he accomplished. He seems shy and quiet, and does not seem very confident. I am not sure he is really ready to be promoted." That creates the perception.

Linda: There is an English philosopher that said, "There are things known, and there are things unknown, and in between are the doors of perception." As a global thought leader on leadership, what is most significant for leaders of teams with global reach and diverse cultures to consider in how they open or close the doors of perception.

Maya: I think that a lot of time that people simply create a perception because of things that they do not know or things that they do not know that they do not know. Working across cultures, working globally, a lot of the time, the tasks are very similar for the leaders, but the gaps are just so much bigger and so much wider. There is so much room for error and so much room for misperception.

Linda: What is something that the person, either the leader or the person them self should be thinking about specifically on how they open or close that door?

Maya: For the leader to close that gap and to open or close that door, it is important to communicate; "Communicate, communicate, communicate." It is very important for the leader to not only be transparent about what they think, how they feel, and how they see the situation, but then they also must really be open to listen and understand the other person's perspective so that hopefully the gap can be narrowed and then the perception will be more accurate. It is important also for both sides to state your intentions clearly and repeatedly. Very often, the wrong perception occurs when we do not understand the other person's intention. When we do not understand where the other person is coming from, we tend to assume the worst in many cases.

I recommend that you always check your assumption and as a leader, ask for feedback. Check in to make sure that what you are saying is clearly understood and interpreted by the other person so that there is not misperception or misinterpretation of your intention or your message. They just really need to understand others perspectives to minimize misunderstandings.

Linda: What is your view in how diligent leaders are globally with managing perception? I am hearing some of that insight with how you are answering just now. Is there anything you would add to that in terms of diligence?

Maya: Sure. I would suggest that with global leaders; they have to first education themselves. In order to work effectively with global teams and global business partners, you have to develop cultural intelligence and you must develop the ability to adapt to different situations. Now, what I mean by cultural intelligence is that we have to first understand how to have a good self-awareness of your own behavior, your own value systems, your own cultural backgrounds and who you are. The second step is to have a good understanding of the culture or the people that you are working with: Understand their perspective, where they are coming from, and what their core values are.
Now, once we understand that, then we can then start to build a bridge between who I am and who you are. Then we can develop better understanding, better appreciation, and we can also start building stronger long term relationships and trust. Then we can eliminate some of the potential misperceptions.

Linda: One of the skills that I speak to in the book is about how we are always trying to create the chapters in the book of our story; that we can rip out chapters three, four, and eight and still know the plot, generally speaking. But it is only through really putting all the chapters in the book and being aware of the context, that you can have the full story.

Maya: I agree, I agree. Context is everything. We must be able to see the big picture, and not just looking at the different signs or different cues. Then we just start to create our own stories. Really to be able to understand the whole story, it is really helpful.

Linda: Another of the skills in the book is about knowing the roles perception as those in a cooking show. Over the years I have found that one of the most powerful metaphors I have been able to really explain. My realization was inspired from my having 400 cookbooks of my own.

Maya: I love to collect cookbooks myself.

Linda: The whole thing is if you look at cooking shows, there is the chef cooking, or there might be a team cooking; and there is also the character "the narrator" that explains, "Look at that team over there," and, "Look at this ingredient." The narrator makes you understand the ingredient, why it is powerful, why the show needs to be a show, why the product is something that you want to eat and serve to your team or to the organization. This attribute of understanding that there is two roles of chef and narration; with global leadership, what is important to consider in how a leader narrates the experience to create buy-in and gain momentum?

Maya: This a good analogy. Now, when you are describing the cooking show, and I am a big fan of watching cooking shows when I am not working. It is certainly interesting to see that when the narrator is trying to explain what the chef was doing, was cooking. Then later on, they would interview the chef about their own experience when they were busy cooking the dish, what was it like. Then you can see that sometimes there is a gap there and is not always closely aligned. It is the same thing when we are working in a global environment that it is very helpful for us to have that alignment.

I mentioned earlier about "Communicate, communicate, communicate." It is important to have meaningful conversations with our employees, with our coworkers. They do not have to be every day, but certainly that when you have the chance to connect with them, to have meaningful conversations, ask questions, understand their perspective; those type of conversations can really help you build a stronger relationship and work much more effectively together going forward. It is very important to be able to create those kind of opportunities to connect with people in a much deeper level. That way, I think that peoples' perception can change. Very often, we hear people say, "When I first met you, I thought you were this and that. But then once I get to know you, it completely changed how I think of you." This is the power of perception.

I do like to say, Linda, that when we talk about managing perceptions, people often say to me, "Isn't that manipulative?" I think there is a difference there. If we are managing our perception to help people see who we truly are and to see our authentic self, then you are simply helping people to see you as the real you, and that's not manipulative.

Linda: I'm so glad you brought that up because that is one of the things I speak to, in the fact that you may feel manipulative when you are trying to get somebody to do something; but if you are living up to your highest values where you may feel uncomfortably uncomfortable, we might feel manipulative and phony when we are simply not comfortable or used to it.

Maya: I also think that when we talk about manipulative, is that the underlying meaning is, the implication is that ultimately your agenda is to benefit yourself. There is a selfish agenda, and it is a, "What's in there for me?"

Linda: That is great. One of the things that I have found with perception is that it is important to teach others how to work with us. That we cannot assume that people know how to work with us or that they feel comfortable asking. How do you feel about that in terms of the global environment of perception management?

111

Maya: Yes, and I think the word teach is right. It may or may not work well if what you teach does not align with your action and your behaviors. I think that teaching would not work if the leader does not walk the talk. Leaders need to build trust. They need to create a psychological safety with others and put others at ease. We talk about this term psychological safety, which is based on a new Google study of global teams. They concluded that psychological safety is the number one factor to create positive, effective, high performing teams.

Psychological safety is something that is so critical and it involves two things. One is that there is a conversational turn taking. Everybody gets to talk equally, and everybody gets to have the chance to say what they think and how they feel. The second key factor is the social sensitivity. People are sensitive to how other team members are feeling. I think that for global leaders to be effective, they have to be willing to listen and accept different ideas and really lead by example, is the key factor.

Linda: Perceptions are evolving, changing, and move with events and situations over time. Perception is not usually an instantaneous, just add water situation. One of the skills is taking charge of the bell like with Pavlov's dog. You have to give perception a transition opportunity until the bell is ringing for the other perception. What would you say to that in terms of the global leadership aspect? Particularly in the virtual world? I would like you to comment on the virtual dynamic of that as well.

Maya: Absolutely. I think one of the key challenge for global leaders is to work virtually and to work with people you hardly ever see or never met. You also are working with people from very, very diverse backgrounds. In order for leaders to be able to really engage the global teams, they have to as I mentioned earlier, create those quality moments to have a good, insightful conversation with their employees. It is not just all about work or checking in, "Hey, give me a status report. What's going on? Okay, have you done this? Have you done that? All right, goodbye." That type of interaction does not create cohesiveness. It does not create trust. It does not build effective teamwork. For leaders to really help create these positive perceptions about him or her as a leader, and also help the team work better together, is to have those quality conversations. If you do not have the budget or the means to bring people together physically, do this type of conversation via video calls. That can really help break down some of the barriers and break the ice so people are feeling more comfortable that they are talking to a real person, and they can observe their body language and their surroundings.

When we talk about working across cultures, many, many world cultures are high context culture. By "high context culture" meaning: that when they communicate, they do not just focus on the words that you are using or speaking; they look at the whole context. They look at where you are, if you are at home or are you in the office, or if you are on the train commuting somewhere, or you are driving, or you are in a restaurant. They look at the context, they also look at the relationship you have, and also at the time, how you feel. Are you in a hurry? Are you at ease? Are you happy? Are you upset? They look at the whole context. Then they are strategic about how to communicate with each other because they pay attention. In that case, I think that we can really eliminate a lot of the misperceptions and create positive perception about each other if we pay attention to those little things.

I would like to think of us as having this antenna in our head and that if our antennas are very low, meaning that we do not really pay attention, we just focus on the words we are using and getting the things done, and when we are in a hurry, we do not have time to chit chat. Versus, "I'm paying attention to what's going on. Why is this project delayed? Is something going on at home? Or is there some kind of team conflict among the team members?" The leader needs to really pay attention and have their antenna up. Have your antenna up and really watching and listening and observing, and picking up things that other people do not pick up. That is really a good way to create positive perceptions and also enhance the teamwork.

Linda: We have been talking about perception here for a while. Is there any thought that has not been explored that you just want to throw that into the mix?

Maya: Yes, I think perception is very a powerful thing. People can form their perception often based on how the other person made them feel. People form their perception based on that. Whether they actually know you as a leader or they heard about you, it is how they feel about your action, your behavior and impact on them. Also, perception is reinforced by others, then it can actually become a belief, a strong belief. This can go in either a positive way or a negative way.

Linda: I appreciate you taking time out to share your perspectives, so that I can have people see the real life applications of the skills in PERCEPTION POWER in a the world of global and cross-cultural leadership. Many thanks!

INTERVIEW: Greg Loudoun Insights on Perception in Entrepreneurship

I met Greg Loudoun over 10 years ago at a Leadership Conference. He was an extraordinary thought leader when I met him and was immersed in the world of enabling entrepreneurs to make a quantum jump in their businesses. Of all the people I have met in the field of leadership, he stands ten-fold above all of them in the world of entrepreneurship. We have remained friends and colleagues for the 10 years since meeting at the conference.

Please note that the interview has been edited.

Linda: We have known each other for over a decade. The reader is getting to know you perhaps for the first time. So why don't you give them a brief overview of your breadth of thought leadership and expertise with entrepreneurs.

Greg: I started my own entrepreneurial business in the IT servicing and support market in Australia in 1997. This business grew to over 450 people in less than 2 years.
Also, 30 years ago I started my own consultancy business called Acumen International focused on helping entrepreneurs across the world to think strategically and grow their businesses by out-thinking the competition versus peddling harder or out pricing the competition. Our clients range from start-up businesses through to corporations with turnovers exceeding $2b. We have worked with executive leadership teams in a diverse pool of industries

including construction, ITC, manufacturing, professional services, distribution, engineering and architecture.

Over the past 20 years I have been a thought leader in all aspects of strategic leadership and agility. We have developed a program called Executive Acumen that through collaboration provides CEOs and entrepreneurial leaders access to thought leadership and proven methods to create strategic agility and engage the talent both within their teams and from external stakeholders. Linda (author/interviewer) is one of our outstanding thought leaders and I am privileged to call her a dear friend as well as to learn from and with her.

Linda: In your view, how significant is perception in the equation of success of generating significant positive momentum with entrepreneurs?

Greg: Perception is the synthesis of thinking and the trigger for focused action. Entrepreneurs often start their businesses with an instinct supported by assumptions focused through refined mindsets. Unfortunately the power of perception is sometimes blinded through the seduction of "BUSYNESS;" from which entrepreneurs consider the time to search for acuity and insights as indulgence rather than a high return investment that enables agility. This mindset has the capacity to distort their own perception and result in disengagement with the people they have the privilege to lead and inspire to greatness.

Linda: "There are things known and there are things unknown, and in between are the doors of perception." As an expert in entrepreneurship, what is most significant for leaders of entrepreneurial organizations and teams to consider with how they open or close the doors of perception?

Greg: Most successful entrepreneurs and their businesses thrive on ambiguity and challenge predictability. They engage their people to capture the unique thinking capacity and capability through disparate perspectives and unleash collective perception power. They go beyond thinking outside the box to creating new business models and therefore a new box.

To open the doors of Perception entrepreneurial leaders must change mindsets to value collaboration rather than individual performance, search for the answers to ambiguous challenges by exploration rather than reductionist thinking, value each persons' unique perspective and integrate them into a shared Perception.

Linda: What is your view on how entrepreneurs are managing perception? And, to what degree?

Greg: The new generation of entrepreneurs often take a narrow view and attempt to succeed by a focus on market reach without considering the problem to be solved by different customers and creating richness through value creation. This fast, micro focused approach limits the opportunity to create and capture perception power. The talent pool is often like thinking and lacks diversity of perspective, opportunity to share and explore thinking dimensions and the belief that the search for perception power is an investment rather than an indulgence.

An example of this narrow focus is the aspiring APP development business that works on an exercises monitor and fails to see the problem to be solved is balanced lifestyle. The micro-focus restricts effective listening and engagement of potential customers as well as members of the development team. This short lived firm is replaced by a team that embraces the value creation from Perception Power and agile leadership to see the need for an integrated approach that links sleep, exercise, nutrition, and stress management.

Linda: In looking through the content of Perception Power, what do you feel the opportunity is for entrepreneurs to leverage these skills?

Greg: I believe that Perception Power if developed and used wisely through engagement and collaboration is the missing piece between me too businesses searching for reach vs those that create true value and sustainable business growth with resilience/agility. Skill ONE – Ensuring the story is heard is my opinion is the game breaker.

The future must be described though a compelling story that resonates with all stakeholders and demographics. It must be authentic and meaningful and compelling. Leaders must manage perception via the art of storytelling in their own language and not "word-smithed." They must tell a story that impacts on how people think, act, react and feel. This is the essence of crafting a cultural architecture. Great and bold strategy requires Perception Power to be executed.

Knowing the right numbers is also critical and they need to trigger ownership, accountability and a meaningful story both rear vision and even more important, future vision.

Linda: If you think of perception roles in terms of a cooking show, where you are cooking up the perception of what is being experienced or achieved. There are two roles of the chef and the narrator. With entrepreneurship, what is important to consider in how a leader narrates the experience to create buy-in and gain momentum?

Greg: The chef executes the vision of the narrator but brings the moment alive. Leaders must create the story to trigger followership horsepower. If the narrator doesn't get the story right and meaningful, the performance will be random and incomplete. It's like the conductor and the orchestra – they both need each other to create a fantastic performance but the trust co-dependency is critical. Perception Power enables and captures the magic of this trust bond.

Linda: What are your insights on how entrepreneurs need to teach customers and other business professionals proactively to react to them?

Greg: Entrepreneurs always have to "punch above their weight" as they rarely have access to the bandwidth of resources, capability and capacity necessary to maintain the winners' edge. Perception power is about building these engagement relationships so that the entrepreneur and therefore their business is a valued source of competitive edge for the customer not just a vendor or lowest cost supplier.

Linda: Thanks Greg for the opportunity to interview you and give perspective to the readers on how Perception Power is critical to entrepreneurs.

ABOUT THE AUTHOR

Linda Shaffer-Vanaria's personal mission is to help people and organizations be calibrated and ready to engage uncertainty and disruption with clarity, confidence, and comfort. She is a #1 international bestselling author, keynote speaker, thought leader, and executive coach. Among others, she has been interviewed by World Champion Quarterback, Joe Theismann; the original shark on Shark Tank, Kevin Harrington, and the Queen of Selling on T.V., Forbes Riley.

Linda's goal is to empower leaders to face the breadth of challenges in today's volatile world with courage, ingenuity, and strategic focus. From coaching and consulting 1,000+ leaders in a breadth of global organizations such as Royal Dutch Shell, ABB, Life Technologies, Acumen International Australia, and The Defense Logistics Agency, Linda has found that there is an increasing need and hunger for precise approaches to strategic thinking and decisive action.

Linda acquired and honed her expertise in Edge Performance from her 20+ year career and experiences as one of the first women U.S. Navy Test Pilots and Squadron Commanders. Linda understands firsthand what it means to push the edge. Her signature story, 2.5 Seconds to Live: A Leaders Guide, recounts her personal experience in surviving the crash of a high performance military jet airplane in which after pulling the airplane's ejection handle to initiate seat ejection, the seat did not fire, with Linda finding herself still inside a doomed airplane, literally with only a few seconds remaining until impact. This experience inspired and motivated Linda to create models and approaches to help leaders with the Edge experiences they face in their careers and daily lives.

Following Linda's tenure as a Naval Officer, she worked as a member of an elite team of leadership and performance development professionals building global leadership bench-strength and business acumen capability throughout the reaches of a global oil company. She then established her own consulting company, Enterprise Coaching of Carlsbad, and is currently celebrating 15+ years of service to global organizations and leaders.

Linda's outside interests span Dachshunds, Harley Davidson motorcycles, artwork, cooking, and family time.

HIRING LINDA TO SPEAK AND CONSULT

In addition to PERCEPTION POWER, Linda has also authored PILOTING YOUR EDGE as well as having written chapters or been interviewed as a leadership expert in several other books. PERCEPTION POWER skills are critical for leaders, teams and organizations to master to optimize their competitive advantage as well as their resilience and influence day to day. You can reach out to hire Linda for your next event or leadership development needs at Linda@LindaShaffer-Vanaria.com
Or contact her on her cell phone at +1 760.272.6730.

Some of the things we could work on together are:
1. Building your Perception Power Action Plan
2. Facilitating your team in emerging their Perception Power
3. Crystalizing your mindset to integrate Perception Power with your cross organizational strategies
4. Leveraging Perception Power to cascade your organizational and leadership philosophies
5. Q&A session to take questions and provide insight on how to leverage Perception Power skills in their unique circumstances
6. Virtual Group Coaching
7. Other Edge Performance growth and development needs

Made in the USA
Las Vegas, NV
03 August 2022

52537972R00085